GRIT DON'T QUIT

get back up and keep going:
learning from Paul's example

BIBLE STUDY GUIDE + STREAMING VIDEO

Bianca Juárez Olthoff

Harper*Christian*
Resources

Grit Don't Quit Bible Study Guide

© 2023 by Bianca Juárez Olthoff

Published in Grand Rapids, Michigan, by HarperChristian Resources. HarperChristian Resources is a registered trademark of HarperCollins Christian Publishing, Inc.

Requests for information should be sent to customercare@harpercollins.com.

ISBN 978-0-310-16255-1 (softcover)
ISBN 978-0-310-16256-8 (ebook)

HarperChristian Resources titles may be purchased in bulk for church, business, fundraising, or ministry use. For information, please e-mail ResourceSpecialist@ChurchSource.com.

Author is represented by the literary agency of The Fedd Agency, Inc., P. O. Box 341973, Austin, Texas, 78734.

First Printing August 2023 / Printed in the United States of America

CONTENTS

A Note from Bianca 5

The Down-Low (FAQs) 9

Where My Leaders At? (Leader Guide) 14

SESSION 1

Sweet Surrender 16

SESSION 2

Listen Up 52

SESSION 3

New Rebellion 82

SESSION 4

The Who 116

SESSION 5

Straighten Your Crown 144

About the Author 173

A NOTE FROM BIANCA

Hi Friend!

If we were sitting next to each other, we would DEFINITELY be talking too loud, laughing too hard, and most likely end our conversation with a hug. So though we aren't near each other, I'm SO glad you're joining me in this study.

First, I am beyond grateful that you have chosen to take this journey. I have prayed endlessly for your experience inside these pages. And I am honored to be with you along the way. Second, I am *so* proud of you for engaging in this opportunity to drop some baggage, to turn from your hang-ups or struggles, and to take the next step in the right direction.

You may be thinking: *Not another feel-good message on determination and not giving up.* But this ain't that, friends. This is a study looking to those who have come before us and overcome the same life circumstances we still encounter so we can follow in their footsteps with full confidence of grit being worth it.

If you're participating in this study, it's likely you feel like you're on the brink of break down. That you're at the bottom of a mountain with no gas in your emotional or physical tank to climb it. Or maybe you just need this important reminder.

But here's a message straight from the throne of God: *You can do it.*

You can take on any challenge, persevere through any disappointment, and hurdle over any obstacle. *But you can't do it alone.* With the immeasurable and miraculous power given to us through God's Holy Spirit, there is *nothing* we can go through on this earth that can beat us. How do I know?

Girl, because I've been there.

I've dealt with:

▶ Caring for a parent with brain cancer

▶ Bad breakups

▶ Comparison to my twin sister

▶ Being single through my twenties

▶ Being broke

▶ Step-parenting

▶ Exhausting jobs

▶ Questioning my calling

Looking back at each of these seasons, I can clearly see the hand of God moving me through to the other side of those situations.

In this study, we're going to draw largely on the life and ministry of one of the Bible's grittiest men—the Apostle Paul (you may also know him as my Bible boyfriend). Through studying Paul's words, actions, and life, we will discover a path through setbacks that promises to get us through *anything*. But if you want a preview, here's what's coming:

After cruelly oppressing followers of Jesus, Paul (still Saul at that time) had a radical encounter with God on the road to Damascus. God called him out and gave him specific directions on what to do next. When it came time for him to start a ministry and spread the gospel, Paul was met with skepticism, judgment, and fear from believers who didn't think he was an *actual* Christian because of his past persecution of believers (Acts 9:26). And that's just the tip of the iceberg! As he pressed toward his calling, Paul was also mocked, beaten, imprisoned, starved, shipwrecked, bitten by a snake, stranded, and abandoned by partners in ministry.

Yet through all his trauma, trials, and tribulation, Paul refused to give up. He showed perseverance, resilience, and grit, leading countless to the cross and fulfilling the mighty calling on his life.

We'll also dig deeper into Scripture to learn from the lives of some lesser-known men and women who showed grit that didn't quit. Through their stories and my own, we're going to unpack five steps we can all take toward a life marked by godly grit:

Step One: Fully surrender to God's will.

Step Two: Listen to the voice of God.

Step Three: Don't conform to the pattern of this world.

Step Four: Lean into the "*who*" when you want to ask "why."

Step Five: Keep your eye on the prize—a crown that lasts forever.

I will keep it real with you, and I ask you to do the same. This won't work if you don't do the work honestly and vulnerably. I'm boldly going to ask that we show up as friends (even if we don't know each other yet)! This is an overused phrase, but I'm going to use it: You are safe here. I pray these pages are a refuge *and* a recharge for you and your faith. Bring your mess, bring your failures, bring your secret struggles, bring your give-up moments, and let's learn how to persevere through the impossible together.

My heart's desire for you is that in the days and weeks ahead, your mindset, your faith, and your entire life is flooded with wisdom, strength, and growth. I desperately want a life of grit for you—and know it's already yours for the taking! I pray you receive tools through this Bible study to live a life that's far more than just *surviving*, but a life of *victory* and a life of *conquering*.

I'm not telling you it's going to be easy. But I am telling you that it's going to be worth it.

Are you ready for transformation? All it takes is an open mind, willing heart, and commitment to *not give up.*

If you're with me, keep reading!

THE DOWN-LOW
(FAQs)

Note: These are the types of sections in books and studies I'm tempted to skip. But . . . DON'T BE ME. Please, read this section carefully, as it contains helpful information that will enhance your experience and the group's experience!

WHAT'S THE DEAL?

This study guide is designed to be used in conjunction with the five-session *Grit Don't Quit* video teaching. Questions in this study guide will take ideas, stories, and topics discussed in the videos to the next level and lead you into deeper personal work to cement what you have learned.

This whole study is designed as a complement to my book, *Grit Don't Quit.* To make the most of your experience, I suggest reading the book in full before beginning this study. But if you haven't made your way through *Grit Don't Quit* just yet, don't panic. You're still going to benefit from our time together.

HOW MANY PEOPLE CAN PARTICIPATE?

The *Grit Don't Quit* video curriculum is set up to be experienced in a group setting like a Bible study, a class during a weekend gathering, or in a small group. If you're not participating in any community like that right now, invite a few of your girlfriends over and make it happen. (And keep it up, because cultivating a supportive Christian community is *key* to maintaining godly grit for the long haul!)

After viewing each video session, you and your group members will participate in a time of discussion. Ideally, discussion groups should be no larger than twelve people. But feel free to max out your space and break up into smaller groups to discuss. (I'm not trying to limit you, sis!)

Finally, someone should be designated as the group leader for each session. This can be the same person, or you can take turns. There are specific notes for the leader on page 14 in this book that must be read before beginning the study.

WHAT DO I NEED TO COMPLETE THIS STUDY?

Well, if you're holding this participant guide, you've already got one resource checked off the list! I recommend each participant have her own. You know, so you can confess your deepest darkest secrets in these pages. Kidding! (Or am I?)

I would also suggest bringing a Bible along with you or having a Bible App loaded and ready to roll. You'll also want a pen or something to take notes with (Read: an excuse to buy pretty pens!).

Each session in this guide includes video outline notes, group discussion questions, and in-between personal Bible study to deepen your learning between group meetings.

Participants are also strongly encouraged to have a copy of the *Grit Don't Quit* book. This guide will refer to the book often, and it will also include all quotes referenced from the book. These excerpts will be best understood within the context of the entire book.

All said, this study guide with streaming videos + this book will give you the most ideal experience.

HOW LONG SHOULD EACH SESSION TAKE TO COMPLETE?

Plan to meet for about an hour—maybe a little longer if you wanna graze the snack table before starting the video. If you're the leader, check out the video length before each session and determine how long you'll have for each remaining section. I'd also place a pretty star beside any of the questions you absolutely want to ask in case you begin running short on time during the discussion section.

WHAT DOES THE INDIVIDUAL STUDY LOOK LIKE?

There are five "Getting Gritty" days for participants to complete on their own. These entries should take about 15–20 minutes to complete. Not only will these Getting Gritty days continue the grit-don't-quit conversation throughout the week, but they will also help you develop a consistent habit of reading God's Word regularly (if that isn't already your thing).

Now, I know these Getting Gritty days sound like "homework." That's because they sort of *are.* Just like showing up at church every Sunday won't change your life without a daily commitment to act, this study won't help you become gritty unless you put in the work.

The Getting Gritty sections will include:

PAUSE

Before you start each Getting Gritty section, spend a few moments preparing your heart by either speaking to or listening to God. This will position your heart and mind to receive and respond!

PLAN

I've included a few bullets that will help you plan your time of study. These will include a reminder about the time commitment, a "heads up" about how the Scripture passage connects to the topic for the week, and a space for you to write what *you* are hoping to do with this time.

READ

I hope this isn't a surprise, but there will be Scripture reading each day. This entire study is deeply rooted in God's Word, so be ready to open your Bibles and soak up some knowledge.

RESPOND

It's imperative to bring God's Word into our everyday lives. These personal questions will help you evaluate where you are in your journey toward godly grit and will aid in applying Scripture to your decision making day-to-day.

ACTIVITY

This in an activity designed to help you process the teaching to make it your own. It may include a prompt for prayer, a suggestion for journaling, or even a topic to sit and ponder. This section takes what you've learned one step further to help you personalize and apply it.

CHALLENGE

These are actions steps to take that turn the ideas we discuss together into tools to practice on your own. Everything you talk about will amount to nada unless it's put into action. This is an opportunity to stretch yourself, to take some risks, and to do the hard work required to maintain godly grit.

REFLECTION

At the end of each Personal Study week, these questions will contextualize the entire week's experience and emphasize the points you don't want to forget.

REMEMBER . . . NO SHAME!

If you're anything like me, you have a hardy dose of legalism simmering just below the surface. But I'm here to tell you there is *no* space for nonsense in this study. If you can't get through any or all of the prompts in the Deeper sections, please don't quit showing up for the study. I know you're busy, but I do pray you prioritize this time in your life and work hard to participate at whatever capacity you're able. I want something *big* for you through this journey. But for that to happen, you've got to show up.

If you're ready to commit to this journey together, read the paragraph below out loud:

"I solemnly swear to openly evaluate places in my life where I'm stuck—spaces where I want to give up. I am committed to persevering and completing this study because I am resilient, and I want to get back up every time I'm down."

If you're willing to give this study all the grit you can muster, I promise you will get so much more in return. Now, let's make it official by signing your name below to indicate your pledge to finishing this study just as strong as you start it!

Signed:_____   Date: _____

Signed:_____   Date: _____

WHERE MY LEADERS AT?
(Leader Guide)

Sis, you're a hero.

Whether you're a rookie in the study-leadership game or you're a seasoned veteran, you are choosing to facilitate discussions that will change lives. That's an honor, but it's also a responsibility. My prayer is that through your leadership, you are doubly blessed and that your faith is increased exponentially.

The goal for you is to be a spark—a spark to conversation, a spark to introspection, and a spark to community. You've heard Katy Perry's song, *Firework*, right? That's you. Sparks flying! This doesn't necessarily mean that you have to have a particularly outgoing personality. Just be willing to *go first*.

If you're still a little hesitant to throw your name out there as facilitator, here's a breakdown of what's required to be successful:

1. **Put in the work ahead of time.** Be prepared. That means you *have* to do the reading ahead of time. Trying to cram it all in fifteen minutes before everyone walks in the door will not cut it in this study. If the room fills with silence after the video plays, it's up to you to *spark* a group discussion. Ideally, you'll also have read the entirety of the *Grit Don't Quit* book as well. Also, review discussion questions before each session and decide which ones you really want to discuss that are more specifically representative of things your group is dealing with. Take notes in advance that stood out to you and circle the questions you have chosen not to miss. Give yourself every advantage right on the study guide pages to keep the conversation moving and to share insight the Lord put on your heart and mind as you prepared in advance.

2. **Be vulnerable.** Your group members will mirror your level of vulnerability. This may mean you have to jump first, but I'm confident you won't find yourself there alone. While I certainly don't expect you to open with your deepest, darkest secrets (in fact, that's probably a bad idea), you may have to be the first one to share honestly.

3. **Stay on topic.** Yes, trash TV can be amazing. But get those conversations out of the way while you're chips-and-dipping. Once you start the video, you are the captain of that conversation ship. Steer the dialogue toward the content as much as possible. If you have a particularly chatty group, plan thirty additional minutes at the top of the study to catch up.

   Another important note: The most dangerous dynamic to have in a study isn't someone who doesn't speak at all, but someone who speaks TOO MUCH. As a leader, I'd set a "share" time limit—something like three minutes each share to keep the conversation moving.

4. **"I don't know," is a great response.** You're not going to have all the answers. (Who does?) If a question is raised that you can't answer, feel empowered to say, "I don't know. But I'll find out!"

Prayer, prayer, and more prayer. This is your most important commitment. Pray for your group members by name. Pray for yourself, that God would give you wisdom and courage to dig in, get gritty, and lead fearlessly. With His help, there's nothing you can't do!

SESSION GOAL

Understand how
godly grit begins

by fully
surrendering
to His will.

Session 1

SWEET SURRENDER

STEP ONE
Fully surrender to God's will.

SUGGESTED READING
Chapters 1 and 2 of *Grit Don't Quit*

"And I want to be clear: living a life of grit isn't about success. In its simplest and rawest form, resilience is the ability to show up, endure pain, press on, and keep going—even if you're not winning. This applies to personal failures, unemployment, addiction, relationships, dieting, and every other struggle that is part of the human experience."

—*GRIT DON'T QUIT*, PAGE 14

> In him we were also chosen, having been predestined according to the plan of him who works out everything in conformity with the purpose of his will.
>
> **—EPHESIANS 1:11**

INTRODUCTION

Have you ever heard the phrase, *Raising the white flag of surrender?* Soldiers have been raising the white flags of capitulation for thousands of years. Ancient Roman philosopher Tacitus even wrote about raised white flags following the Vitellian forces' defeat in the Second Battle of Cremona in 69 A.D. I'm not a history buff, and I have no idea what happened at the Second Battle of Cremona, but isn't it wild to think that a tradition like raising a white flag in surrender is something still practiced in combat today?

Maybe you're wondering what "surrender" has to do with "grit." After all, this study is about NOT giving up—isn't "surrendering" like "giving up"? Maybe not. Today, Bianca's going to teach us about the link between grit and surrender, using Scripture and stories from her own life. Surrender is powerful. Surrender changes every dynamic. Where there was once strife and death, surrender brings calm and peace. Raising your own white flag can have the same effect. When it comes to your relationship with God, surrender is *not* the same as defeat. In fact, it's the exact opposite. Surrender means *hope.* Surrender also acknowledges the obvious: In a battle against our will and God's? God's the winner every time anyway.

WATCH THE SESSION ONE VIDEO
(stream video or use DVD)

VIDEO OUTLINE QUESTIONS

As you watch the Session One video, please follow along with the outline. It is meant to help you stay engaged, spark thoughts or questions, and to point out the prevailing themes in each session. As you watch, I encourage you to also take notes or write down points you'd like to follow up on.

If you're the type of person who needs to fill in every blank or answer every question, don't let these guiding questions distract you from the purposeful content on each video session. They are simply meant to contextualize the video, helping to focus and direct your thoughts.

▷ Perseverance is doing something despite difficulty or delay in achieving success.

▷ Endurance is the determination to keep moving forward toward your desired goal despite external challenges or internal weariness.

> Grit is the ability to persevere in pursuing a future
> goal over a long period of time and not giving up.
> It is having the stamina. It is sticking with your future
> day in, day out. Not just for the week, not just for
> the month, but for years, and working really hard to
> make that future a reality. Grit is living life
> like it's a marathon, not a sprint.
>
> **—ANGELA DUCKWORTH**

▶ Paul was a man with influence, power, and zeal before he met Jesus. Paul despised Christians—to death.

▶ Acts 8:3 describes Paul pre-Christ.

▶ Acts 9:6–20 describes Paul after-Christ.

▶ When we live disconnected from the Holy Spirit, we can move outside of the will of God real quick.

▶ God told Paul to "Get up and go." Paul obeyed and got back up.

▶ Showing GRIT is fully surrendering to God's will.

▶ If God wanted you to be where you think you should be, you would already be there.

▶ If we don't have it, that doesn't mean we won't ever get it. It's just not now.

DISCUSSION QUESTIONS

Friend, let's dig into the teaching. This is an opportunity to grow together and to get honest! If those words terrify you, that's OK. Take a deep breath and remember that you're going to *get* what you *give* in this study. For us to experience life change, we need to be real about where we are in our lives.

Use these questions as a guide for group conversation. Make sure to leave enough time at the end to talk about the next meeting, share prayer requests, and spend a few minutes in prayer.

Conversation Starter: Do you have a story about literally falling, tripping, or being brought to your knees? If so, share it with the group.

1. Like Bianca mentioned, the Bible never uses the word "grit," but the concept is definitely there in Scripture. Words like "perseverance" and "endurance" appear throughout the Bible. Do any particular passages, stories, or verses come to your mind as we're talking about grit, perseverance, and endurance?

2. Have a volunteer read Jesus' words to Paul in Acts 9:4-6. What stands out to you about the words that Jesus used to speak to Paul? What stands out to you about Paul's words and actions in response to Jesus?

3. God aligned Paul with His will in a dramatic way. What does Paul's conversion story help us understand about grit and God's timing?

4. Think of a few adjectives that could describe Paul both before AND after his conversion (look at Acts 8:3 again if you need to). For example, even before his conversion, he was determined. What else was in Paul's character and person? What kind of raw material was God working with?

5. Ephesians 1:11 says, "In him we were also chosen, having been predestined according to the plan of him who works out everything in conformity with the purpose of his will." When we obey God, we are telling Him that His plan is more important than our plan. How does obedience give us the ability to show grit?

6. Give an example of a time you were doing everything "right," but weren't getting the results you wanted or thought you deserved? How did it make you feel about God?

7. What's the difference between success and resiliency? Think about this: what is the main goal of a person who is "successful"? Is it different than the main goal of a person who is "resilient"?

8. Let's close with questions from the video: What do you need to surrender today in order to align yourself more closely to the will of God? And if you're on your knees right now, on your own dusty road to Damascus, will you show grit to get back up?

Before Next Time: We're going to wrap up this discussion with a few reminders about the next meeting and about the personal study.

Our next meeting, time and place:

In this week's personal study, we'll read more biblical stories of surrender and walk through practical ways to live out surrender in our own lives.

What I'm hoping to get out of the personal study:

For an overview of what the personal study is going to look like, turn to The Down Low (FAQs) on page 11 and read the answer to the question: **What does the individual study look like?**

Leader Note: Close out the session by asking if anyone has a specific prayer request to share with the group. Then, lead the group in a prayer to close. If you feel led, you can also ask someone else in the group to lead the closing prayer. Feel free to use the prayer below to get started.

Lord, we are so thankful that You've gathered us together. In obedience, we want to fully surrender to Your will in every part of our lives. Grit isn't something we can manage on our own, so please inspire our hearts as we look to Your Word this week. We want to give ourselves to You completely.

Amen

Session 1

SWEET SURRENDER

PERSONAL STUDY

Getting Gritty

Participants are to complete the following questions at home, ideally over the course of five different days. **If there are any questions you did not get to during the Group Discussion, I encourage you to work through those during the at-home study time.**

"When we find ourselves falling over life's hurdles, it's easy to want to stay down. We might even get angry with God because we're convinced our way is the best way. But if we decide to adhere to what God whispers to us after we've been knocked down, I believe it will help us remember our calling."

—GRIT DON'T QUIT, PAGE 25

DAY I

Surrender—Take Up Your Cross

PAUSE

Before we start this week of Getting Gritty, take fifteen seconds to ask God to speak to you in ways only He can.

THE PLAN

▶ Prepare to spend at least fifteen minutes total in prayer, reading Scripture, and personal study.

▶ Learn—through the word of God—what surrender looks like in my personal life.

▶ Begin a plan.

READ

Matthew 16:24–27:

> [24] *Then Jesus said to his disciples, "Whoever wants to be my disciple must deny themselves and take up their cross and follow me.* [25] *For whoever wants to save their life[l] will lose it, but whoever loses their life for me will find it.* [26] *What good will it be for someone to gain the whole world, yet forfeit their soul? Or what can anyone give in exchange for their soul?* [27] *For the Son of Man is going to come in his Father's glory with his angels, and then he will reward each person according to what they have done."*

In your own handwriting, write out Matthew 16:24–25.

In verse 24, Jesus tells His disciples two things:

1. They must deny themselves

2. They must take up their crosses and follow Him.

These two commands help us to understand what it looks like to surrender our lives to God. The first command is fairly simple to understand—deny yourself. Deny your flesh, deny your sinful tendencies, deny your personal preference and pleasure over what needs to be done and who is most important (God). Basically, resist doing what you want over what God asks, demands, or wills.

But the second is a bit more complex to understand: "take up your cross." We hear this phrase a lot in Christianity—in sermons, podcasts, and books, but what does it really mean to take up your cross?

For Christ, the cross was His most vulnerable moment. The cross was His most painful moment. The cross is where Jesus was most exposed. The cross is where the very life of Jesus was given up. In a similar way, Jesus asks us to "take up your cross" and acknowledge our own vulnerabilities and fears and weaknesses and to willingly expose them as evidence of following Him.

Both commands comprise the biblical definition of "sweet" surrender.

Many of us (me included) can find *that* level of vulnerability uncomfortable. We avoid exposure—being seen—at great cost. But our egos will become our stumbling block if we aren't careful, because a failure to admit where we're most human can prevent us from fully surrendering to God's will for our lives.

Maybe this topic is discouraging to you because you've tried surrendering everything to Him before—and yet, here you are, not fully surrendered to God's will. Let me assure you, that's not the expectation for this week: that you'd go from "not surrendered" to "completely surrendered." It's a lifelong process. And that's why we need grit to even consider what surrender should look like in our lives.

If we can find the grit to bear our own crosses—to own our shameful ways and embarrassing rebellion and to claim our inability to do and be all we want to be recognized as, to humble ourselves claiming our need for a Savior—we can "save our lives" by losing them. Each time we take up our cross, we keep moving toward Him in surrender. And there's the promise of a great reward for each person who does—being in the perfect and peaceful will of God!

RESPOND

1. In verse 25, Jesus describes two different ways of living. Use three of your own words to describe each of those two paths. What are the ultimate results of those two different paths?

2. In Matthew 16:24–27, Jesus gives commands, makes promises, and asks questions. Which of these commands, promises, and questions make you feel hopeful? Do any of them confuse you? List any other immediate responses you have to these verses.

3. What actions or mindset changes would have to take place for you to follow Christ, living fully surrendered to Him?

4. How would your life look if you denied yourself and took up your cross to follow Jesus? What would be difficult about that? What would be easy?

ACTIVITY

I want to take us old school with a hymn. Pull out your phone or laptop and tune into Judson Van DeVenter's *I Surrender All*. It's a simple song, but as you start making a list of some qualities that need to change, I want music to remind you of truth. Hymns might not be your fav style of music, fine. But put on some kind of worship music with the theme of *surrender*. Then make a list of your character traits and qualities that you need to surrender to Jesus. Maybe you tend to be prideful. Maybe you're not the *greatest* listener. Maybe it's difficult for you to release control to someone else—even God. Maybe you have trouble keeping your mouth shut when you know you should! Whatever you try to make up for with your own power and knowledge, expose those things in writing before God. *This* is what it means to take up our cross.

--   --

--   --

--   --

CHALLENGE

Evaluate the list you made—the areas where you need Christ *the most*. First, know that you are covered in the forgiveness and grace of Jesus. *That's* why His cross existed in the first place! But now that you've made yourself vulnerable before God, write a short note to God asking Him to help you shoulder the load of *your* cross. Tell Him that you'd rather lose your life in Him than gain the entire world. Finally, end your session by thanking God for His work on the cross.

DAY 2

Surrender—Submit Yourself

PAUSE

Before diving into God's Word, pause and state one thing you are grateful to God for.

THE PLAN

▶ Prepare to spend at least ten minutes total in prayer, reading Scripture, and personal study.

▶ Recognize some of my stumbling blocks to surrender.

▶ Begin a plan.

READ

James 4:7–10:

> ⁷ *Submit yourselves, then, to God. Resist the devil, and he will flee from you.* ⁸ *Come near to God and he will come near to you. Wash your hands, you sinners, and purify your hearts, you double-minded.* ⁹ *Grieve, mourn and wail. Change your laughter to mourning and your joy to gloom.* ¹⁰ *Humble yourselves before the Lord, and he will lift you up.*

In your own handwriting, write James 4:7.

_____

_____

_____

If you know anything about the children of Israel, you probably know two things:

1. They were God's chosen people.

2. They were stubborn as all get-out.

On their way to the Promised Land, the Israelites wandered in the desert for forty years—*forty*—because of their reluctance to fully submit and surrender to God. We learn from the story of the Israelites that there's a price to be paid when we fail to submit. And I don't know about you, but I haven't got forty *days* to spare—much less forty years!

Fast forward hundreds of years later to James' words on submitting to Christ.

In the first verse of his book, James addresses "the twelve tribes scattered among the nations." He's writing to other Jews who would have been very familiar with the Psalms and Prophecies of the Old Testament, and he references Old Testament Scriptures throughut the five chapters. Just to get a sense of this, look up Psalm 24:4 and Psalm 73:28, and then look at James 5:8 again. James was both deeply rooted in Jewish tradition and committed to Jesus—who was his *brother.*

I don't know if you've ever had to take orders from a sibling, but I imagine James did not love the idea of being under the authority of his brother. And yet, because of the proof James saw of Jesus' divinity, not only was he able to surrender and submit to Jesus as his leader, but he was also moved to encourage others to do the same.

Based on his own relationship with Jesus and his deep knowledge of his faith, James gave followers of Christ two suggestions on how to submit to God:

1. Resist the devil (avoiding sin).

2. Purify your hearts (repentance).

Some Christians get uncomfortable talking about the devil, but the Bible promises us that we have a very real enemy in Satan. Like God, Satan has an agenda for our lives. But it's not one you nor I want to live out. Through a gritty resistance to sin and purifying our hearts with repentance, we are promised that the Lord will lift us up, setting our feet on His perfect plan for our lives.

RESPOND

1. James uses powerful imperatives in every verse of this passage—he tells his readers to "submit," "resist," "come near," "purify," and even "grieve." Choose three of James's commands. Write out the whole phrases, and align each command with a gritty response. For example, for the command, "Wash your hands, you sinners," a gritty response could be "confess my sins to someone I trust."

2. Repentance means a deep commitment to change our future actions or mindsets. Can you honestly say that you have repented of the sin in your life? If not, what might need to change in order to answer that question differently?

ACTIVITY

Are there certain people you spend time with or certain places you spend time in that typically lead you to sin? I'm not indicating that a person is the enemy, but perhaps the enemy is using them to make you stumble. Make a list of those people and places. Looking at the list, is there anything these people and places have in common? (For example, maybe they lead you to comparison and envy, or overspending, or making unwise choices.)

Becoming more aware of our tendencies and habits will only make our resolve to resist the devil stronger and more consistent.

CHALLENGE

Identify at least one person or place from the list you made that you can work to avoid this week. Commit to God to resist the enemy. Pray and ask God's Holy Spirit to give you the self-control to resist the devil—especially as it relates to what you wrote down. Now, fold up the paper and complete a ceremonial act of "surrendering" it/them to God. Burn it, shred it, toss it in the trash—anything that demonstrates its removal from your life.

Through staying true to this commitment, you are demonstrating true repentance, one of the sweetest acts of surrender.

DAY 3

Surrender—For the Sake of the Gospel

PAUSE

Close your eyes and count to ten slowly. Calm your mind before starting today's reading.

THE PLAN

▶ Prepare to spend at least ten minutes total in prayer, reading Scripture, and personal study.

▶ Read about how Paul lived out his surrender with grit, years after the road to Damascus.

▶ Begin a plan.

READ

1 Corinthians 9:1–23, ESV:

> *Am I not free? Am I not an apostle? Have I not seen Jesus our Lord? Are not you my workmanship in the Lord?* **2** *If to others I am not an apostle, at least I am to you, for you are the seal of my apostleship in the Lord.*

> **3** *This is my defense to those who would examine me.* **4** *Do we not have the right to eat and drink?* **5** *Do we not have the right to take along a believing wife, as do the other apostles and the brothers of the Lord and Cephas?* **6** *Or is it only Barnabas and I who have no right to refrain from working for a living?* **7** *Who serves as a soldier at his own expense? Who plants a vineyard without eating any of its fruit? Or who tends a flock without getting some of the milk?*

> **8** *Do I say these things on human authority? Does not the Law say the same?* **9** *For it is written in the Law of Moses, "You shall not muzzle an ox when it treads out the grain." Is it for oxen that God is concerned?* **10** *Does he not certainly speak for our sake? It was written for our sake, because the plowman should plow in hope and the thresher thresh in hope of sharing in*

35

the crop. **11** If we have sown spiritual things among you, is it too much if we reap material things from you? **12** If others share this rightful claim on you, do not we even more?

Nevertheless, we have not made use of this right, but we endure anything rather than put an obstacle in the way of the gospel of Christ. **13** Do you not know that those who are employed in the temple service get their food from the temple, and those who serve at the altar share in the sacrificial offerings? **14** In the same way, the Lord commanded that those who proclaim the gospel should get their living by the gospel.

15 But I have made no use of any of these rights, nor am I writing these things to secure any such provision. For I would rather die than have anyone deprive me of my ground for boasting. **16** For if I preach the gospel, that gives me no ground for boasting. For necessity is laid upon me. Woe to me if I do not preach the gospel! **17** For if I do this of my own will, I have a reward, but if not of my own will, I am still entrusted with a stewardship. **18** What then is my reward? That in my preaching I may present the gospel free of charge, so as not to make full use of my right in the gospel.

19 For though I am free from all, I have made myself a servant to all, that I might win more of them. **20** To the Jews I became as a Jew, in order to win Jews. To those under the law I became as one under the law (though not being myself under the law) that I might win those under the law. **21** To those outside the law I became as one outside the law (not being outside the law of God but under the law of Christ) that I might win those outside the law. **22** To the weak I became weak, that I might win the weak. I have become all things to all people, that by all means I might save some. **23** I do it all for the sake of the gospel, that I may share with them in its blessings.

In your own handwriting, write out 1 Corinthians 9:12.

You know I couldn't wait much longer to bring up the one and only Apostle Paul.

In these passages, we see that Paul's authority and rights as an apostle were being brought into question by some at the church in Corinth. (And if you think *this* explanation is long-winded, you should read 2 Corinthians 10–13, where Paul goes into even greater detail to defend his calling.)

Not only does Paul point out that he saw the resurrected Christ with his own eyes, but that the church of Corinth itself is proof of his calling. His answer to those who intend to examine him are that he has denied himself even the most basic rights that anyone in ministry might have to enjoy: a wife, a home, a salary. Paul says he doesn't permit himself to possess those things so that he may "present the gospel free of charge, so as not to make full use of my right in the gospel."

In other words, Paul has given over every aspect of his entire life in order to stay focused on the gospel. Talk about surrender!

Paul wasn't distracted by the material things of this world, neither was he distracted by philosophical positions that might sidetrack his effectiveness in the Kingdom of God. For the Jews, he became a Jew. For those under the law, he became like one under the law. Most believe that Paul was eventually martyred. (Something tells me that's exactly how he'd have wanted to go!) Paul's grit was such that he almost ceased to exist outside of his laser-sharp focus on winning souls to Jesus.

Paul's surrender may land him on the "extreme" end of submission to Christ, but surely the reward he experienced in heaven was even more so.

RESPOND

1. In verse 3, Paul tells his readers, "This is my defense to those who would examine me." Paul was an expert on the law of Moses, and he knew how to pull together an airtight defense. When Paul brings up the law about oxen in verse 9, what comparison is he making?

2. In verse 18, Paul describes his reward. What reward is he after, and how does his denial of his rights relate to this reward?

3. Considering all you know about Paul, why do you think his level of surrender was so extreme, even compared to some of the other apostles'?

4. What was the ultimate result of Paul's surrender, not just in his life, but in the lives of others too?

5. Not everyone can be Paul. Paul was hardcore. (That's why I love him!) But we can become more *like* Paul by living for Christ in new and meaningful ways. What can you "give up" for the sake of the gospel? What are some comparative aspects of your life you could surrender? Complete the chart below.

PAUL'S SURRENDER	YOUR SURRENDER
Did not take a wife.	
Did not work a regular job.	
Became a servant to all.	

ACTIVITY

Would you be willing to surrender your response to Christ today? Spend a few moments writing down a commitment pledge to God—Paul's defense included several areas of his life, like his relationships, his money, his work, his rights, and his reputation. He was willing to go the unconvential route in everything. Choose one or two of these areas—or a different area of life inspired by Paul's defense—to pray about right now. How is God calling you toward surrender? Include what you're willing to surrender and how much. For example, if you're thinking about relationships, you could write: "I am committed to spending one hour a week investing in a new believer. I will begin on [START DATE] through [END DATE]."

CHALLENGE

Choose one person who you can begin investing in using your time, energy, or talent. Maybe it's someone in one season of life you've already been through. Reach out personally, face-to-face, and show that person you're thinking of them. Ask them if there's anything specific you can be praying for. Follow up. Be in this person's life during whatever season she is in. Surrender *time* and *effort* in order to make it possible!

Surrendering to God in this way leads us to our greatest assignment—making disciples of Jesus Christ.

DAY 4

Surrender—Where You Go, I Will Go

PAUSE

Take three long breaths by inhaling for four seconds, holding for four seconds, exhaling for four seconds. Repeat three times.

THE PLAN

▶ Prepare to spend at least ten minutes total in prayer, reading Scripture, and personal study.

▶ Find inspiration in Ruth's story of grit and surrender.

▶ Begin a plan.

READ

Ruth 1:3–18:

> ³ *Now Elimelek, Naomi's husband, died, and she was left with her two sons.* ⁴ *They married Moabite women, one named Orpah and the other Ruth. After they had lived there about ten years,* ⁵ *both Mahlon and Kilion also died, and Naomi was left without her two sons and her husband.*
>
> ⁶ *When Naomi heard in Moab that the Lord had come to the aid of his people by providing food for them, she and her daughters-in-law prepared to return home from there.* ⁷ *With her two daughters-in-law she left the place where she had been living and set out on the road that would take them back to the land of Judah.*
>
> ⁸ *Then Naomi said to her two daughters-in-law, "Go back, each of you, to your mother's home. May the LORD show you kindness, as you have shown kindness to your dead husbands and to me.* ⁹ *May the LORD grant that each of you will find rest in the home of another husband."*

Then she kissed them goodbye and they wept aloud **10** and said to her, "We will go back with you to your people."

11 But Naomi said, "Return home, my daughters. Why would you come with me? Am I going to have any more sons, who could become your husbands? **12** Return home, my daughters; I am too old to have another husband. Even if I thought there was still hope for me—even if I had a husband tonight and then gave birth to sons— **13** would you wait until they grew up? Would you remain unmarried for them? No, my daughters. It is more bitter for me than for you, because the LORD's hand has turned against me!"

14 At this they wept aloud again. Then Orpah kissed her mother-in-law goodbye, but Ruth clung to her.

15 "Look," said Naomi, "your sister-in-law is going back to her people and her gods. Go back with her."

16 But Ruth replied, "Don't urge me to leave you or to turn back from you. Where you go I will go, and where you stay I will stay. Your people will be my people and your God my God. **17** Where you die I will die, and there I will be buried. May the LORD deal with me, be it ever so severely, if even death separates you and me." **18** When Naomi realized that Ruth was determined to go with her, she stopped urging her.

WRITE

In your own handwriting, write out Ruth 1:16–18:

Ruth had made up her mind—she wouldn't desert her mother-in-law. Ruth had recently lost her own husband and was on her way to a foreign land with foreign people. To return home wouldn't have necessarily been *wrong,* but Ruth's gritty determination to stay by Naomi's side reflected the depth of Ruth's character and loyalty.

Ruth surrendered what was comfortable and familiar to do what was right, which included turning away from her home, Moab, and the Moabite idols, and instead worshiping Naomi's God—the one true God.

In the end, Ruth met Boaz, a wealthy man with whom she found favor, and married. She went on to become King David's great-grandmother and is named in Jesus' family lineage! Ruth's legacy of grit began with surrender and continues still today.

RESPOND

1. According to verse 9, what is Naomi's hope for her daughters-in-law? How is this hope eventually answered?

2. What does Naomi say in verse 13? How does Ruth's response—which is the opposite of Orpah's—demonstrate grit? What do the examples of these two sisters show you about surrender and grit in the face of others' discouragement and fear?

3. Have you ever received horrible news on top of horrible news? How did you respond? Had you been Ruth, what would have been your first response to the death of your husband and the news you were moving away from home?

4. What did Ruth's surrender to God's will do for her? For Naomi? For Boaz? For us today?

ACTIVITY

It's tempting for us to excuse "bad" behavior when we're going through a painful experience. "I'm just going through something," we'll say. But that's not what Ruth did. She was backed into a corner, vulnerable, and at risk. But she didn't lash out. She chose the more difficult thing—to surrender her will in order to do what was right.

Can you think of a time when you treated someone poorly because you were in emotional pain or distress? Spend a few minutes talking to God about that interaction. Ask Him to forgive you. Ask Him to give you strength the next time you're in a similar situation to make the more difficult choice—surrender.

CHALLENGE

If you are still in touch with the person (or people) you thought of in the previous activity, consider sending them a message or even taking them to lunch. Apologize for the way you handled yourself. Ask for their forgiveness, even if they are no longer upset with you. Even if they don't remember the specific situation! Asking for forgiveness is one of the most powerful forms of surrender!

DAY 5

Surrender—I Have Come to Do Your Will

PAUSE

Start today's reading by spending a few moments thanking Jesus for the ultimate sacrifice He made for you, laying down his life, spilling His blood, and conquering sin once and for all!

THE PLAN

▶ Prepare to spend at least ten minutes total in prayer, reading Scripture, and personal study.

▶ Relate Christ's ultimate surrender to my daily acts of surrender.

▶ Begin a plan.

READ

Hebrews 10:1–10:

> *The law is only a shadow of the good things that are coming—not the realities themselves. For this reason it can never, by the same sacrifices repeated endlessly year after year, make perfect those who draw near to worship.* ² *Otherwise, would they not have stopped being offered? For the worshipers would have been cleansed once for all, and would no longer have felt guilty for their sins.* ³ *But those sacrifices are an annual reminder of sins.* ⁴ *It is impossible for the blood of bulls and goats to take away sins.*
>
>> ⁵ *Therefore, when Christ came into the world, he said:*
>> *"Sacrifice and offering you did not desire,*
>>> *but a body you prepared for me;*
>> ⁶ *with burnt offerings and sin offerings*
>>> *you were not pleased.*
>> ⁷ *Then I said, 'Here I am—it is written about me in the scroll—*
>>> *I have come to do your will, my God.'"*

8 *First he said, "Sacrifices and offerings, burnt offerings and sin offerings you did not desire, nor were you pleased with them"—though they were offered in accordance with the law. **9** Then he said, "Here I am, I have come to do your will." He sets aside the first to establish the second. **10** And by that will, we have been made holy through the sacrifice of the body of Jesus Christ once for all.*

WRITE

In your own handwriting, write out Hebrews 10:10.

_____

_____

_____

Before Jesus' death and resurrection, believers had only the law by which to be cleansed of their sin. The law only provided for highly ritualistic sacrifices and burnt offerings that had to be performed over and over again. But even these offerings of sacrifice were not enough to restore humanity to a right relationship with God.

But with Jesus' sacrifice on Calvary, the law was made the mere shadow of a past of separation from the Father. Through His death, Jesus paid the penalty for humanity's sins, and made it possible to be reconciled with God. This act of sacrificial love is the ultimate expression of God's grace and mercy to us. Through Jesus' sacrifice, we can receive complete forgiveness for our sins, *and* be in right standing with God. The blood of our Savior is *all* that can cleanse and make us whole once and for all. Now, we no longer have to feel guilty for our sins. We no longer have to make sacrifices or burnt offerings. Once we repent, our sin is separated from us as far as the east is from the west (Psalm 103:12).

Jesus' sacrifice is the greatest act of surrender in all of history.

RESPOND

1. Verse 1 says "the law is only a shadow of the good things that are coming." If the annual sacrifice is the "shadow," what is the "good thing coming"—the reality—that corresponds with the law about animal sacrifices?

2. What does God want instead of sacrifice, and how did Jesus live up to His Father's desire?

3. How does Christ's sacrifice pave the way for your surrender?

4. If you had lived under the law pre-crucifixion, how would you have felt about having to make sacrifices and offerings to receive forgiveness for your sins? I know for me, I'd have been making sacrifices every hour on the hour just to make sure it "took." Can you relate? Or might you have been so overwhelmed with getting it "right" that you would have avoided the process altogether?

5. How does knowing Jesus' sacrifice is enough for your permanent and eternal forgiveness change how you view yourself and your sin?

ACTIVITY

Jesus said, "Here I am—it is written about me in the scroll—I have come to do your will, my God." In other words, "I'm going to show grit. I'm going to persevere, regardless of what God tells me to do. Not my will, but His be done." That's *gritty* surrender modeled to us by Jesus Christ Himself.

Spend a few moments in prayer. Ask God what His will is for you *right now*. Then, spend some time journaling His response to you. If you aren't accustomed to "hearing" from God this way, just write down what you feel in your spirit. No one is going to read your words and say, "God didn't tell you *that!*" Just rely on His Holy Spirit to speak to you and guide your journaling time.

CHALLENGE

Looking at what you journaled, find scriptural support for what you believe God's will for you is. Find at least 2–3 Scripture references that confirm what you heard Him speak to you. If you need help, grab your Bible and check out the index for Scriptures or hop on Google and type in *Bible verses on* _____ .

Now that you have heard God speak into your life, your only job is to respond, "Here I am and I'm ready to do your will."

REFLECTION

In Session 1, you read biblical examples of surrender—Paul and Ruth— and heard wisdom on denial and submission from James and from Christ Himself. You also thought through practical ways to live out surrender in your own life.

Reflect on:

Which example of surrender that I read this week sticks out the most in my mind—why is that example meaningful to me?

_____

_____

_____

_____

What similarities did I see between Paul and the other biblical examples who showed grit?

_____

_____

_____

_____

How have I grown spiritually—how have I practiced surrender this week?

_____

_____

_____

_____

Has my perspective on Jesus shifted this week? How?

_____

_____

_____

_____

What have I learned about living a fully surrendered life?

_____

_____

_____

_____

SESSION GOAL

Unpack reasons we might be holding the Holy Spirit at bay,

and commit to connecting or reconnecting with the Holy Spirit— our Advocate and our avenue to godly grit.

Session 2

LISTEN UP

STEP TWO
Learn to listen to the voice of God.

SUGGESTED READING
Chapters 3, 4, and 5 of *Grit Don't Quit*

> *Though I don't hear an audible voice of God, the Holy Spirit leads me, guides me, and empowers me. Jesus promised us that He wouldn't abandon us; He would leave us an Advocate, the Holy Spirit, who will lead us and empower us to do things not in our strength but in His strength (John 14:16–21). The Holy Spirit is our guide and our comforter, and He gives us power. Maybe the reason that Peter said the Holy Spirit is a gift (Acts 2:38) is because having a guide and a comforter is literally the greatest gift in life. Why wouldn't everyone want this gift?*

— GRIT DON'T QUIT, PAGE 68

> " Then Ananias went to the house and entered it. Placing
> his hands on Saul, he said, "Brother Saul, the Lord—Jesus,
> who appeared to you on the road as you were coming
> here—has sent me so that you may see again and
> be filled with the Holy Spirit. "
>
> **—ACTS 9:17**

INTRODUCTION

Not too long ago I was watching a survival show where all contestants were dropped in some forlorn location and they each got to pick a weapon or survival tool. While most contestants picked weaponry like a sword or a spear, one guy picked duct tape. DUCT TAPE.

I immediately became a couch commentator. I was like, "What a fool! Are you serious? How dumb!"

I lived to eat my words.

This man used duct tape to make a hut, formed a bed with leaves, and made various forms of weaponry using sharp rocks and wood. This guy even went on to survive the ENTIRE challenge—because of his duct tape!

This got me thinking. What would I take with me into battle? What would my survival tool be? Better yet, what do we all have at our disposal that we aren't using like we could to show grit during life's battles? What is within our access that we have been sleeping on?

Let me tell you today—it's better than duct tape.

The most effective survival tool that we should be armed with daily is the Holy Spirit of God—His very presence and voice. To be able to show grit for the challenges we will face, all we have to do is invite Him into our lives, listen, and obey.

WATCH THE SESSION TWO VIDEO
(stream video or use DVD)

VIDEO OUTLINE QUESTIONS

As you watch the Session Two video, please follow along with the outline. It is meant to help you stay engaged, spark thoughts or questions, and to point out the prevailing themes in each session. As you watch, I encourage you to also take notes or write down points you'd like to follow up on.

▶ In Acts 2:38, what does Peter call the Holy Spirit?

▶ John 14:16–17 describes the Holy Spirit's role in our lives. It says: "And I will ask the Father, and he will give you another advocate to help you and be with you forever—the Spirit of truth. The world cannot accept him, because it neither sees him nor knows him. But you know him, for he lives with you and will be in you." Define advocate.

▶ In the teaching video I say, "I want to set the record straight: the Holy Spirit is not a ghost, not fire, not wind, or a dove. He's often symbolized by these things, but they're not Him." So, what (or who) is the Holy Spirit?

▶ Like Ananias, has God ever told you to "GO" and you wanted to respond "NO!"?

▶ What does hearing from God have to do with maintaining grit?

DISCUSSION QUESTIONS

Friends, let's dig into Bianca's teaching. This is an opportunity to grow together and to get honest. If those words terrify you, that's OK. Take a deep breath and remember that you're going to get what you *give* in this study. For us to experience life change, we need to be real about where we are in our lives.

Use these questions as a guide for group conversation. Make sure to leave enough time at the end to share prayer requests and spend a few minutes in prayer.

Conversation Starter: If you were to be dropped into a remote location and could only bring one survival tool with you, what would *you* bring?

1. What kinds of gritty actions does the Holy Spirit help Christians take? The video mentioned Matthew 5:44; Romans 12:14; Matthew 6:14; Romans 8:31. What other biblical commands can you think of that—at first glance—feel unapproachable or impossible?

2. What happened right after Paul's conversion on the road to Damascus? How did Paul encounter the Holy Spirit (Acts 9:17–18)?

3. In the Scripture used in today's teaching (Acts 9:17–18; Acts 18:9–10), how do you see the Holy Spirit working on individual and communal levels?

4. How does Paul respond to the promptings of the Holy Spirit? What can we learn about grit from his responses?

5. Can you relate to any of the three reasons given to explain why some of us don't tap into the power of the Holy Spirit? (The idea that He's a "creepy" ghost or spirit, the Holy Spirit is unknown to you, or that in your experience, the Holy Spirit has been manipulated or abused.)

6. The Holy Spirit does more than help us distinguish "good" from "evil." It helps us distinguish "good" from "almost good" and "God's will" from "my will." What's at stake for you if you fail to learn to listen to the voice of God?

7. God doesn't speak to be heard—He speaks to be obeyed.

8. What proof do we have that listening to the voice of God is our most powerful tool when it comes to maintaining grit over time?

9. What is the Holy Spirit saying to you, right now, in this season of life?

Before Next Time: We're going to wrap up this discussion with a few reminders about the next meeting and about the personal study.

Our next meeting, time and place:

In this week's personal study, we'll read Scripture that will teach us more about the Holy Spirit and take practical steps toward leaning into its power.

What I'm hoping to get out of the personal study:

Leader Note: Close out the session by asking if anyone has a specific prayer request to share with the group. Then, lead the group in a prayer to close. If you feel led, you can also ask someone else in the group to lead the closing prayer. Feel free to use the prayer below to get you started, or use your own prayer.

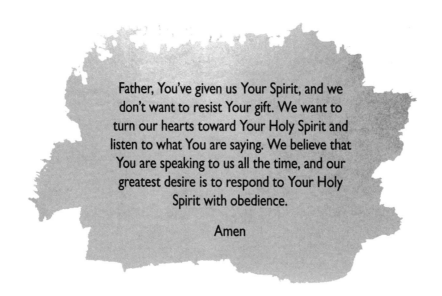

Father, You've given us Your Spirit, and we don't want to resist Your gift. We want to turn our hearts toward Your Holy Spirit and listen to what You are saying. We believe that You are speaking to us all the time, and our greatest desire is to respond to Your Holy Spirit with obedience.

Amen

Session 2

LISTEN UP

PERSONAL STUDY
Getting Gritty

Participants are to complete the following questions at home, ideally over the course of five different days. **If there are any questions you did not get to during the Group Discussion, I encourage you to work through those during the at-home study time.**

> ". . . all the greatness, grandeur, and glory that is in the fullness of God the Father is in the person of the Holy Spirit."

—*GRIT DON'T QUIT,* PAGE 69

DAY 1

Listen Up—Demolish Strongholds

PAUSE

Before we start this week of homework, take fifteen seconds to ask God to speak to you in ways only He can.

THE PLAN

- ▶ Prepare to spend at least _____ minutes total in prayer, reading Scripture, and personal study.

- ▶ Reconsider the power and purpose of prayer.

- ▶ Begin a plan.

READ

2 Corinthians 10:3–5:

> [3] For though we live in the world, we do not wage war as the world does. [4] The weapons we fight with are not the weapons of the world. On the contrary, they have divine power to demolish strongholds. [5] We demolish arguments and every pretension that sets itself up against the knowledge of God, and we take captive every thought to make it obedient to Christ.

WRITE

In your own handwriting, write out 2 Corinthians 10:4.

_____

_____

_____

Does your mind ever race to the worst-case scenario?

Mine too. I can be really creative with my runaway thoughts, so I need a reminder of God's power over all circumstances. I know I can't be the only one! Read Paul's words again within the context of our lives:

For though we live in the world (here on earth), we do not wage war as the world does (there are currently wars in Ukraine, Russia, South Sudan, Syria). The weapons we fight with are not the weapons of the world (tanks, guns, armory). On the contrary, we have divine power to demolish strongholds (in Greek, an acumoura: a fortress to keep people in and enemies out; or in our case, the enemy keeps us trapped in lies and holds the truth at bay). We demolish arguments and every pretension that sets itself up against the knowledge of God, and we take captive every thought to make it obedient to Christ.

It's so crazy to me how often even Christians undervalue and discount the power of prayer. You see it all the time. Tragedy strikes and people say, "Oh my gosh. All we can do now is pray."

I can almost imagine God going, "And you think that's nothing?" The God who can move mountains, the God who could raise the dead, the God who could heal the sick and open blind eyes and all you can do is pray? No, prayer is powerful, and as followers of Jesus, we have to recognize that prayer is our first option, not our last resort.

Prayer is how we connect to the Spirit of God. It's how we commune with Him, learn from Him, and where we often hear from Him. When we choose to turn to prayer instead of running "worst-case scenario" playbacks through our head, we tap into perseverance, resilience, and grit.

If you're struggling to hear the voice of God in your life, my first question for you is: How is your prayer life?

RESPOND

1. If prayer is our weapon, what are some specific examples of the weapons of this world? According to Paul, what are these weapons lacking?

2. Describe your current prayer life. When do you pray? Where? How often and for how long? Would you like to see this time change in any way?

3. When you pray, do you ever invite in the Holy Spirit? Do you sit and listen for the voice of God, or do you spend most of the time talking? How would you like to see your practice of listening during your prayer time change?

4. How do we know that prayer is *anything* but a last resort? How has prayer benefited your life or the lives of others?

ACTIVITY

Prayer is our direct channel to God's Holy Spirit. But often, we do most (or all) of the talking. Spend a few minutes outside today and invite the Holy Spirit to join you. (If you can't go outside, find a nice nook somewhere with a window.) Often, nature helps us connect with God in a deeper, more meaningful way. (Plus, you can't be distracted by the piles of laundry on the floor.) Once outside, allow your mind to relax. Take in the beauty of God's creation. When your heart has quieted, ask God to speak to you. When you return home, write in your journal what you heard God speak.

CHALLENGE

Schedule "listening" time with God into your daily calendar. Maybe start with three minutes in the morning and work your way up. Set a reminder on your phone. Invite a friend to do the same and hold each other accountable. Remember, giving God the opportunity to speak is critical to gaining godly grit.

DAY 2

Advocate

PAUSE

Before diving into God's Word, pause and state one thing you are grateful to God for.

THE PLAN

▶ Prepare to spend at least _____ minutes total in prayer, reading Scripture, and personal study.

▶ Read what Jesus said about the Father's reasons for sending the Holy Spirit. Begin a plan.

READ

John 14:25–26:

> [25] *"All this I have spoken while still with you.* [26] *But the Advocate, the Holy Spirit, whom the Father will send in my name, will teach you all things and will remind you of everything I have said to you.*

WRITE

In your own handwriting, write out John 14:26.

_____

_____

_____

_____

When you have something to take care of or critical information to share, you want to make sure it's understood. However, when time is critical, sometimes you can't help but squeeze in *All the Things*. If you've ever left someone in charge at work as you were heading out on vacation, or dropped the kids off at the sitter while heading out on a date, you know what I'm talking about. As you were walking out the door, all the pertinent information just came tumbling out—only what was necessary for success and survival.

As Jesus was preparing to be crucified, time was infinitely precious. He needed to give His disciples the most important information before He was nailed to the cross to ensure the success and survival of His followers. One of Jesus' last promises is that God the Father would send the Holy Spirit, who would do two things: (1) teach us all things, and (2) remind us of everything Jesus already taught.

One of the most powerful aspects of the Holy Spirit is that He is the revealer of what's *true*. If you have the Holy Spirit inside of you, you cannot be comfortable with sin. But if you ignore the Holy Spirit for long enough . . . His voice and conviction will begin to fade. The distance between us and God will increase, and our capacity for grit will decrease.

RESPOND

1. Consider the verses (John 14:25–26) again. What action or actions does Jesus associate with each of the members of the Trinity? How are these actions interrelated?

2. Why do you think Jesus took what little time He had left on earth to teach His disciples about the Holy Spirit?

3. Have you ever ignored the voice of the Holy Spirit or His conviction? What happened?

4. Is your heart soft toward the Holy Spirit right now? Or have you distanced yourself from Him? If you don't feel a divine connection to God's Spirit, what can you do to change that?

ACTIVITY

Is there a situation in your life right now that you're struggling to find the *truth* in? Where you're wondering what the right thing to do is? Journal about it. Tell God what's going on. Then, tell God how you feel about it. When you're finished, spend a few moments in prayer. You can read the words you wrote to God, or you can simply speak from the heart. Cry out to Him, He hears you.

CHALLENGE

Ask God's Holy Spirit to reveal what's true and right about your circumstance through the Word of God. (You can go to a passage you are aware of that addresses your circumstance, ask a friend who is familiar with the Word of God to help you, or Google some verses around the topic you are researching.) Whether through a Scripture or Bible commentary, what did you learn? Sit and listen for His response. If it doesn't come right away, repeat this activity and challenge every day until He does.

DAY 3

Listen UP—Filled with the Holy Spirit

PAUSE

Close your eyes and count to ten slowly. Calm your mind before starting today's reading.

THE PLAN

▶ Prepare to spend at least _____ minutes total in prayer, reading Scripture, and personal study.

▶ See an example of the Holy Spirit in action through Jesus' followers.

▶ Begin a plan.

READ

Acts 4:1–10:

> The priests and the captain of the temple guard and the Sadducees came up to Peter and John while they were speaking to the people. ² They were greatly disturbed because the apostles were teaching the people, proclaiming in Jesus the resurrection of the dead. ³ They seized Peter and John and, because it was evening, they put them in jail until the next day. ⁴ But many who heard the message believed; so the number of men who believed grew to about five thousand.
>
> ⁵ The next day the rulers, the elders and the teachers of the law met in Jerusalem. ⁶ Annas the high priest was there, and so were Caiaphas, John, Alexander and others of the high priest's family. ⁷ They had Peter and John brought before them and began to question them: "By what power or what name did you do this?"

8 Then Peter, filled with the Holy Spirit, said to them: "Rulers and elders of the people! 9 If we are being called to account today for an act of kindness shown to a man who was lame and are being asked how he was healed, 10 then know this, you and all the people of Israel: It is by the name of Jesus Christ of Nazareth, whom you crucified but whom God raised from the dead, that this man stands before you healed."

WRITE

In your own handwriting, write out Acts 4:9–10.

_____

_____

_____

_____

_____

In these passages, we see Peter and John arrested and thrown in jail for preaching the gospel. As someone involved in a jail ministry, I have been inside the walls of prison, and it is *not* a place I want to be in voluntarily. But also, inside those walls, I have met some of the bravest, most devoted, God-loving people I've ever met.

But if I were dragged before a judge and jury whom I knew hated my God, when asked "by what power" I preached the gospel, I might hesitate to respond with anything other than respect and decorum.

Not Peter, though.

When filled with the Holy Spirit, Peter answered that very question by essentially saying, "My power comes from Jesus Christ of Nazareth. You know, the man you murdered? Spoiler alert: He beat death, hell, and the grave to prove He is the *very* person you said He isn't."

Peter didn't just respond in truth, he responded *boldly*. His mortal life was at stake, but through the godly grit of the Holy Spirit, Peter stood in holy defiance before the men who held his fate in their hands.

RESPOND

1. Think of a few other "Peter" stories from the gospels. Has he changed since the resurrection of Jesus and the coming of the Holy Spirit? If so, how?

2. Would you describe yourself as a "bold" person? Why or why not? Give some examples of people you know who are bold.

3. If you had been Peter, dragged before a group of men waiting to throw you in jail or kill you, would you have been able to show the same holy defiance? Really think about it. Is there anything different about the Holy Spirit in us and the Holy Spirit in Peter?

4. Is there an area in your life, a relationship, or a situation you're in right now that God wants you to respond to boldly? With godly grit? Describe that situation. What would holy defiance look like for you?

ACTIVITY

It's time to break out the worship music and come boldly before the throne of God. Often, I feel the most boldness while worshiping the Father through song.

Find your favorite worship track. If you don't have one, you can borrow one of mine: "Break Every Chain" by Tasha Cobbs. You may have to go out to your car to do it, but crank that song up as loud as your ears can take. Play it as many times as it takes to feel God's Holy Spirit within you.

Then, invite God's Holy Spirit to make you *bold*. As bold as Peter—as bold as Paul. There is *no* difference in the Holy Spirit within them and the Holy Spirit within you. Boldness gives us grit, and grit gets us through.

CHALLENGE

Through the power of the Holy Spirit, take a bold step of holy defiance this week. Maybe it's ending a relationship. Maybe it's starting one! Maybe you need to apply for that job or ask for that promotion. It may be a difficult conversation you've been dreading, but you know it needs to happen. Ask God's Holy Spirit to go before you and make it happen!

DAY 4

Listen Up—Here I Am

PAUSE

Take three long breaths by inhaling for four seconds, holding for four seconds, exhaling for four seconds. Repeat three times.

THE PLAN

▶ Prepare to spend at least _____ minutes total in prayer, reading Scripture, and personal study.

▶ Consider how your surroundings help you hear from the Holy Spirit.

▶ Begin a plan.

READ

1 Samuel 3:1–4:

> The boy Samuel ministered before the LORD under Eli. In those days the word of the LORD was rare; there were not many visions.
>
> 2 One night Eli, whose eyes were becoming so weak that he could barely see, was lying down in his usual place. 3 The lamp of God had not yet gone out, and Samuel was lying down in the house of the LORD, where the ark of God was. 4 Then the LORD called Samuel.
>
> Samuel answered, "Here I am."

WRITE

In your own handwriting, write out 1 Samuel 3:4.

We talked about the story of God speaking audibly to Samuel in this week's video session. But what we didn't unpack was the environment Samuel was in when God spoke.

One of the first things we learn is that "the word of the LORD was rare" during this time. In other words, God wasn't really speaking to people often. So how did Samuel find himself in the position to hear from God? First, he was ministering under the guidance of Eli. He was in service to others. And second, Samuel was literally sleeping in the house of the Lord.

If you've ever met a realtor, you've heard it said that prime real estate is about one thing: location, location, location. And Samuel was in the right location. Not only was Samuel involved in ministry, but his "usual" spot was in God's house.

If we want to align ourselves with the will and voice of God—if we want to open our hearts to the movements of the Holy Spirit—we have to be in the right location. Not just spiritually, but physically as well.

RESPOND

1. Take a moment to consider some of the details of the story of Samuel—for more context, look up verses 1–10 in 1 Samuel 3. Why did Eli need a helper? What time of day did God's call come to Samuel? Did Samuel recognize God's call right away, or did he need help to understand it?

2. Are you involved in any ministry service right now? It doesn't have to be formal—it could be an experience volunteering in a shelter or even dropping off second-hand clothes and toys at a donation center. How does serving others affect our proximity to God? And how does our proximity to God affect our ability to hear His voice?

3. What has your experience in the church been like? Are you involved in regular church attendance right now? Do you believe that making church your "usual" spot has the power to transform your ability to hear from God?

4. If you're not involved in church life right now, take some time to write about why not.

ACTIVITY

Make a list of your "usual" spots—places you often frequent. Maybe it's a restaurant, your workplace, a gym, or a park. Beside each spot, give a rating (1–10) of how likely you are to hear the voice of God there. Write a 1 if it would be very unlikely to hear from God there and 10 if God talks your head off at that place. What have you learned about your usual spots? Do you often put yourself in the right location to hear from God's Holy Spirit? If not, how could you change it up?

(This activity isn't meant to communicate that you can't go certain places. This exercise is simply a tool to help you evaluate where you hear from God and where you don't. But if you have any spots with a "1" beside them, I would consider removing yourself from that environment.)

CHALLENGE

Listen to God's voice and find a way to serve *this* week. Maybe it's dropping off a meal to a friend who is sick or just had a baby. Maybe it's signing up to tell the Bible story in your church's kid's program. Serving others positions our hearts and souls toward God in a way that nothing else can. And if we want to increase the godly grit of hearing from God, serving others is one of the best ways to develop that muscle.

DAY 5

Listen Up—Know His Voice

PAUSE

Take your hand and place it on your heart. Before you dive into the Word, take an emotional temperature. Where is your heart? If it feels pressured, panicked, pursuing other things, ask God to still your heart.

THE PLAN

▶ Spend at least _____ minutes total in prayer, reading Scripture, and personal study.

▶ Identify some distracting voices that might be preventing me from hearing from the Holy Spirit.

▶ Begin a plan.

READ

John 10:1–5:

> "Very truly I tell you Pharisees, anyone who does not enter the sheep pen by the gate, but climbs in by some other way, is a thief and a robber. ² The one who enters by the gate is the shepherd of the sheep. ³ The gatekeeper opens the gate for him, and the sheep listen to his voice. He calls his own sheep by name and leads them out. ⁴ When he has brought out all his own, he goes on ahead of them, and his sheep follow him because they know his voice. ⁵ But they will never follow a stranger; in fact, they will run away from him because they do not recognize a stranger's voice."

WRITE

In your own handwriting, write out John 10:3.

_____

_____

_____

I could pick out my husband's voice in a crowded room from fifty yards away. I'm just *that* familiar with his intonations and cadence. I'm sure he'd say the same about me as well (although that might be because I'm Latina and born loud!). But how familiar are we with the voice of our Shephard? Are we able to follow Him in the darkness by the sound of His voice? Or are we distracted by the voices of strangers?

If you're having trouble hearing from God, don't lose heart. You can become more familiar with the voice of the Father. What does His voice sound like? When and where does He speak to you most often? What types of things does He say?

Prayer isn't the only way we can become more familiar with the voice of God. We can also hear His voice in Scripture.

RESPOND

1. In the passage you read from John, Jesus compares Himself to a shepherd. How does the Good Shepherd treat His sheep—are they familiar with Him or surprised by Him? What actions does the shepherd take that show his trustworthiness to the sheep?

2. Outside of this study, how much time do you typically spend in Bible reading each week?

3. Now, compare that amount of time to the amount of time you spend . . .

On social media

Listening to podcasts

Binge-watching your favorite show

Texting your friends

Shopping online

4. How does the amount of time you spend in the Word of God compare to the amount of time you spend in the word-of-the-world? What kind of changes would you like to see in how much time you spend in God's Word? Are you willing to commit to becoming more familiar with His voice through studying and reading Scripture?

ACTIVITY

Identify some of the other voices in your life—the voices of "strangers." Now, I'm not talking about godly friends and mentors who speak truth. I'm talking about the "outside" voices that can lead us astray. Write down some of those voices below. (You might include: society, social media, politics, our past selves, etc.)

_____   _____

_____   _____

_____   _____

CHALLENGE

Looking at the list above, work through them one by one, asking God's forgiveness for letting those voices be louder than His. Then, find at least one Scripture reference for each "voice" on the list that helps you become more familiar with the voice of God. (If you have six competing voices, find six Scripture references that reveal the character of God.) Choose one or two of those Scripture references and commit them to memory this week.

REFLECTION

Before you begin the next session, spend a few moments reflecting on what you've learned in Session Two about listening to the Holy Spirit.

Reflect on:

Which Scripture passage about the Holy Spirit was the most meaningful to me? Why does it stand out in my mind?

How have I grown spiritually—what practical steps have I taken toward listening to God in my daily life?

What new way of "listening" did my time of study inspire me to try?

What new ideas about the Holy Spirit have I embraced?

_____

_____

_____

_____

_____

What have I learned about listening to the voice of God?

_____

_____

_____

_____

What is one thing I *cannot* forget that I learned during this session?

_____

_____

_____

_____

_____

SESSION GOAL

Define "conformity" and learn why our responses to life's challenges must be different that the world's.

Session 3

NEW REBELLION

STEP THREE
Do not conform to the pattern of this world.

SUGGESTED READING
Chapters 6 and 7 of *Grit Don't Quit*

"When we feel like we are drowning in life or feel like we can't get up from an emotional blow, that's a sign our mental and emotional reserves are depleted. When we experience too many unsolved emotional aggressions or trauma, it can make us more prone to breaking down and less able to quickly recover. How in the world do we bounce back from situations like these? You guessed it: by developing grit and strengthening our resilience."

—*GRIT DON'T QUIT*, PAGE 100

> " Therefore, I urge you, brothers and sisters, in view of God's mercy, to offer your bodies as a living sacrifice, holy and pleasing to God—this is your true and proper worship. Do not conform to the pattern of this world, but be transformed by the renewing of your mind. Then you will be able to test and approve what God's will is—his good, pleasing and perfect will. "
>
> **—ROMANS 12:1–2**

INTRODUCTION

Who is the first person that comes to your mind when you hear the word *rebel*? Is it that kid from your high school who was constantly in and out of detention? Is it those line-cutters at the self-checkout lanes at the grocery store? Or maybe it's James Dean—the rebel without a cause.

I bet the last person who you would relate to rebellion is Jesus. But Jesus was a rebel. He came as a complete afront to the culture and leaders of His day. The Pharisees and religious leaders didn't like Jesus. They didn't like Jesus' friends, either. They looked for any reason to lock them up and throw away the key.

Why? Because Jesus was not like them. He said new things—hopeful things. He called Himself God's Son and offered God's love and forgiveness to everyone—even the Gentiles! Jesus' teachings were radically different from their oppressive and law-driven faith.

Not only did Jesus come to break the patterns of a cruel and cold culture, but Jesus also came as a rebel to darkness. To evil. To our enemy. Jesus was all love, but don't mistake that love for weakness. No, it took guts to be

Jesus. It took *grit* to live the noble, upright, righteous, holy life that Jesus lived. Jesus was rebellious, even in death:

> *Therefore I will give him the many as a portion,*
> *and he will receive the mighty as spoil,*
> *because he willingly submitted to death,*
> *and was counted among the rebels;*
> *yet he bore the sin of many*
> *and interceded for the rebels.*
> —Isaiah 53:12, CSB

As His followers, we are to model the same nonconformity. We are the new rebellion—a people of love in a world of hate, a people of hope in a world of despair, and a people of joy in a world of sorrow.

WATCH THE SESSION THREE VIDEO
(stream video or use DVD)

VIDEO OUTLINE QUESTIONS

As you watch the Session Three video, please follow along with the outline. It is meant to help you stay engaged, spark thoughts or questions, and to point out the prevailing themes in each session. As you watch, I encourage you to also take notes or write down points you'd like to follow up on.

▶ How often do you find yourself thinking, I'm such an idiot! Or, I can't ever get anything right! How could I be so stupid? Would you say those same things to a friend?

▶ When it comes to conformity, are there areas of your life that you find yourself willing to bend or break?

▶ 1 Peter 1:15–16 says, "But just as he who called you is holy, so be holy in all you do; for it is written: 'Be holy, because I am holy.'"

▶ Paul says, "Don't quit!" Renew your mind.

P _____

A _____ your feelings

S _____ the truth

T _____

▶ Philippians 4:11–13: Can you think of anything more countercultural than being content?

▶ Would you say that you are often aware of what you're *really* thinking and feeling?

DISCUSSION QUESTIONS

Friends, let's dig into Bianca's teaching. This is an opportunity to grow together and to get honest! If those words terrify you, that's OK. Take a deep breath and remember that you're going to *get* what you *give* in this study. For us to experience life change, we need to be real about where we are in our lives.

Use these questions as a guide for group conversation. Make sure to leave enough time at the end to share prayer requests and spend a few minutes in prayer.

Conversation Starter: What's the most rebellious thing you've ever done?

1. Can you think of any other biblical "rebels" like Paul—people who did not conform to the patterns of this world even in the face of trials, difficult circumstances, and extraordinary pressures?

2. Like Bianca says in the video, admitting feelings is not a lack of grit—it's an essential part of it. Read the beginning of David's lament in Psalm 22:1–2. Then, look up Matthew 27:46 and Mark 15:34 to see who else showed this kind of grit while suffering.

3. Look up the passage that Bianca mentioned in the video—Ecclesiastes 7—and look through verses 7–10. What other kinds of "conforming" does this passage describe? What kinds of pressures lead to conforming in these ways?

4. What's our world like when it comes to life's hurdles and wrecking-ball moments? What's the cultural response to the trials of life?

5. How would you describe someone who is *holy*. Do you feel like a holy person? Why or why not? Why do you think you hold this opinion of yourself?

6. When it comes to the acronym I gave for renewing your mind, which "letter" would be the most difficult for you and why?

   Acronym:

   P: Pause

   A: Admit your feelings

   S: State the truth

   T: Thankfulness

7. In Philippians 4:11 Paul writes, ". . . for I have learned to be content whatever the circumstances." On a scale of 1 to 10, 1 being not at all content and 10 being very content, how would you rate your level of contentedness right now? What would it take to increase that number?

8. What's one step you can take this week to separate yourself from the patterns of this world?

Before Next Time: We're going to wrap up this discussion with a few reminders about the next meeting and about the personal study.

Our next meeting, time and place:

_____

In this week's personal study, we'll read more Scripture about being like Jesus—not like the world around us—and we'll uncover some places in our hearts where we're conforming to the patterns of this world.

What I'm hoping to get out of the personal study:

Leader Note: Close out the session by asking if anyone has a specific prayer request to share with the group. Then, lead the group in a prayer to close. If you feel led, you can also ask someone else in the group to lead the closing prayer.

Jesus, we want to rebel against the patterns of this world, just like You did. Please open our hearts this week—help us to see the ways we do conform, and give us the grit to start living differently. Your love gives us the power to be different, to be hopeful, and to be perfectly content.

Amen

Session 3

NEW REBELLION

PERSONAL STUDY

Getting Gritty

Participants are to complete the following questions at home, ideally over the course of five different days. **If there are any questions you did not get to during the Group Discussion, I encourage you to work through those during the at-home study time.**

> When we pause and look introspectively, we force ourselves to evaluate the motivations behind our choices, which can reveal the issues that have us stuck.

—*GRIT DON'T QUIT*, PAGE 87

DAY 1

New Rebellion—In View of God's Mercy

PAUSE

Before we start this week of homework, take fifteen seconds to ask God to speak to you in ways only He can.

THE PLAN

▷ Prepare to spend at least _____ minutes total in prayer, reading Scripture, and personal study.

▷ Lean into the "why" of nonconformity—why should I be different than the world?

▷ Begin a plan.

READ

Romans 12:1–2:

> *Therefore, I urge you, brothers and sisters, in view of God's mercy, to offer your bodies as a living sacrifice, holy and pleasing to God—this is your true and proper worship.* ² *Do not conform to the pattern of this world, but be transformed by the renewing of your mind. Then you will be able to test and approve what God's will is—his good, pleasing and perfect will.*

WRITE

In your own handwriting, write out Romans 12:1.

....

....

....

In our video session for this week, we focused on the latter half of that passage: Romans 12:2. But in studying God's Word, we should always be aware of scriptural context that provides us with a deeper understanding of what we're reading.

What's interesting about the context of Romans 12:1 is that it begins with the conjunctive adverb "therefore." In other words, "Because of all this." So, what's the "this" Paul is referring to? Well, it's everything he talked about in Romans prior to chapter 12—*all that Jesus has done for us.* You can replace the word "therefore" with: "Because of all that Jesus has done for us, I urge you, brothers and sisters . . ."

Nonconformity in light of *all* the work Jesus did during His life, on the cross, and through His resurrection does not feel like that big an ask. If Jesus wants nonconformity to the very patterns He came to break, my grit to do so increases when I think about all He's done for me.

RESPOND

1. Paul uses the word "bodies" in verse 1 to describe what Christians' sacrifice should look like. Why do you think he used the word "bodies" instead of "hearts" or "minds"?

2. How does the context of Romans 12:1 change the way you feel about the actions Paul urges us to make in Romans 12:2?

3. What is one of your biggest stumbling blocks to nonconformity? In other words, in what areas of life are you most tempted to conform to the patterns of this world? (Think: worry, comparison, gossip, over spending, over eating, other numbing techniques and unhealthy coping mechanisms, etc.)

4. How might it enhance your life if you were to conform *less* to the ways of this world? Think: spiritually, physically, emotionally.

ACTIVITY

Make a list of all the patterns you see in this world on one side of the page. On the other side, make a list of all Jesus has done for you (think specifically too—what He's done for you personally).

WORLDLY PATTERNS	THE COST OF CONFORMING	JESUS' WORK FOR ME	WHAT I GAIN

Look at the Worldly Patterns column. Beside each pattern listed, write down what conforming to that pattern has cost you or could cost you in the future.

Now, look at the Jesus' Work for Me column. Beside each work listed, write down what you gained from each and what you stand to gain from each in the future.

CHALLENGE

Choose one item from your Wordly Patterns column. What would it look like to resist conformity to this specific pattern? Are you willing to show the grit required to start a new rebellion in your own life against this pattern?

Spend a few minutes in prayer committing to resist this pattern. Find a verse to fight against the worldly pattern, or hold onto Romans 12:2. Ask that God would help you maintain the grit required to resist conforming to this pattern.

DAY 2

New Rebellion—Above All Else

PAUSE

Before diving into God's Word, pause and state one thing you are grateful to God for.

THE PLAN

▶ Prepare to spend at least _____ minutes total in prayer, reading Scripture, and personal study.

▶ Recognize why guarding my heart is so important.

▶ Begin a plan.

READ

Proverbs 4:23:

> Above all else, guard your heart, for everything you do flows from it.

WRITE

In your own handwriting, write out Proverbs 4:23.

_____

_____

_____

_____

Our hearts are the life-sustaining organs in our body. We read a lot about the "heart" in the Bible. In Matthew 6:21 we read, "For where your treasure is, there your heart will be also." In Psalm 37:4 we read, "Take delight in the LORD, and he will give you the desires of your heart." Our hearts matter.

They're the command center or our souls—our mind, our will, and our emotions.

In Proverbs 4:23, we're given a strong warning in regard to our heart: "Above all else, guard your heart." *Above all else, Lord? Not our careers? Not our bank accounts? Not even our ministry? Why?*

Because everything we do flows from our hearts. That's a bold statement, isn't it? But it's true. Even when we don't realize it, our hearts (souls, wills, and minds) are in the driver's seat. This is why change has to come from the heart. Have you ever tried to change your actions without considering what was going on in your heart? You could probably force the change—kicking a bad habit, having a better attitude—for a couple of days, but it didn't stick. That's because it wasn't a heart change. We have to go back to the beginning—we have to know what's going on in those hearts of ours.

What are we thinking?

How are we feeling?

What beliefs do we embrace?

What beliefs do we reject?

All these answers lie in our hearts. When Paul tells us to renew our minds, he's also asking us to renew our hearts. That's what nonconformity does—it opens the eyes of hearts to the will of God. But to get there, we have to focus on the inputs to our heart. What are we putting *into* our souls, wills, and minds? What are failing to put in?

RESPOND

1. Look up Proverbs 4:20–27. In the verses following 4:23, which parts of the body are mentioned? Do you see how the actions of these parts "flow" from the heart—what becomes vulnerable if the heart is not guarded?

2. Relate guarding your heart to having grit—how does understanding what's going on in your heart help you show grit?

3. Let's do a quick heart check! Answer the following questions based on how your heart feels right now.

   What are you thinking? _____

   How are you feeling? _____

   What beliefs do you embrace? _____

   What beliefs do you reject? _____

4. Do you own anything that you have to guard or protect? (House, pet, child, heirloom jewelry, etc.) What lengths do you go to in order to guard or protect it? If you went to the same lengths to guard your heart, how much would your life be different?

ACTIVITY

What people, places, and things does your heart encounter on a regular basis? Jot down a quick list. (Think: music, shows, movies, friends, family relationships, work relationships, repetitive thoughts, etc.)

_____   _____

_____   _____

_____   _____

Looking at your list, how many inputs to your heart are life-giving and God-affirming? Write those down here.

_____

_____

Now, for those that _aren't_ life-giving and God-affirming, how can you guard your heart against them? (This doesn't mean that you avoid them altogether—that's not always possible. But how can you prepare your heart to encounter them?)

CHALLENGE

This week, be vigilant in guarding your heart. Create some kind of physical reminder—a rubber band on your wrist or rock in your pocket. Every time your heart is compromised by fear, anxiety, or pain, or toxicity, let that reminder nudge you to renew your mind and heart by resisting the patterns of this world.

DAY 3

New Rebellion—Father of Lies

PAUSE

Close your eyes and count to ten slowly. Calm your mind before starting today's reading.

THE PLAN

▶ Prepare to spend at least _____ minutes total in prayer, reading Scripture, and personal study.

▶ Acknowledge the enemy's lies and see how they've affected my life.

▶ Begin a plan.

READ

John 8:44:

> *You belong to your father, the devil, and you want to carry out your father's desires. He was a murderer from the beginning, not holding to the truth, for there is no truth in him. When he lies, he speaks his native language, for he is a liar and the father of lies.*

WRITE

In your own handwriting, write out John 8:44.

_____

_____

_____

Friends, we have a very real enemy in Satan. He is a murderer and there is no truth in him. I know I have been the victim of his venomous whispers. As you read in *Grit Don't Quit*, he almost convinced me to quit ministry.

More than once.

You're not good enough.

You don't have what it takes.

You can't do this.

Who would want to follow you?

I'm sure you've experienced similar, painful thoughts. But a critical step in renewing our minds is knowing how to respond to him. That would be easy, if all he did was lie. Do you know what Satan's best trick is? Making our past failures feel like truths today. In other words, "Remember that time that you _____?" You can fill in the blank with whatever screw up you want. We've all had them—and the enemy *thrives* on bringing them back to our memory.

How do we combat *that?* How do we fight against an enemy who knows our deepest, darkest secrets and regrets? When he reminds us of our short-comings and sins, how can we say, "That's a lie!", when we know it's true?

I'm glad you asked, sister. Because I have the perfect comeback to the scumbag. And here it is: "You know what, Satan. You're right. I did do that/say that/fumble that/lost that."

I tell the enemy he's right. But then I remind him of this: "That may be what I did, but that is not who I am."

Then I tell him that I am a child of the Most High God. That I have been bought at a high price and am redeemed and forgiven. That, yes, though I am imperfect on earth, Christ has made me spotless in the eyes of the King who defeated Satan for eternity.

Satan will try to dissolve our grit, but reminding him of who you are as child of God renews your mind . . . and shuts his mouth.

RESPOND

1. In John 8 (starting at verse 31), Jesus is speaking to "the Jews who had believed him." Based on the discussion they're having, these followers believe Him, but they don't see why they need freedom. Read what Jesus says in verse 34. What does Jesus offer us?

2. What lies does Satan like to whisper to you? What past mistakes and failures does he like to remind you of? How have his attacks affected your life?

3. How do you usually respond when Satan taunts and torments you? How can you react differently in the future? What would your life be like if you showed godly grit and renewed your mind instead of giving into the wiles of the enemy?

ACTIVITY

Open your Bibles and find at least five Scripture references that state who you are in Christ Jesus. List them out below. (If you need help finding verses, Google *what the Bible says about me*.)

_____

_____

_____

_____

_____

CHALLENGE

Work to commit the Scripture references you wrote down above to memory. If you have to carry around a sheet of paper or type them out in the Notes app on your phone, do it! The next time the enemy tries to slither up to your ear, you'll be armed to the hilt with a comeback. If a whole verse seems daunting, try personalizing a phrase: "I am justified by his grace!" (that one's from Titus 3:7). The devil hates the word of God, and reminding him of any part of it is a grit move.

"Satan, let me renew *your* mind for a change."

DAY 4

New Rebellion—A Jealous God

PAUSE

Take three long breaths by inhaling for four seconds, holding for four seconds, exhaling for four seconds. Repeat three times.

THE PLAN

▶ Prepare to spend at least _____ minutes total in prayer, reading Scripture, and personal study.

▶ Understand more about idols and God's jealousy.

▶ Begin a plan.

READ

Deuteronomy 5:8–10:

> **8** *"You shall not make for yourself an image in the form of anything in heaven above or on the earth beneath or in the waters below.* **9** *You shall not bow down to them or worship them; for I, the LORD your God, am a jealous God, punishing the children for the sin of the parents to the third and fourth generation of those who hate me,* **10** *but showing love to a thousand generations of those who love me and keep my commandments.*

WRITE

In your own handwriting, write out Deuteronomy 5:9.

Any American Idol fans reading? I watched every single episode of the first season when Kelly Clarkson took home the prize. Outside of that show, the word "idol" isn't one we use a lot in everyday language. But I'm willing to bet that many of us have everyday idols.

God doesn't mince words with how He feels about idols. "You shall not" doesn't leave a lot of wiggle room. According to Him, He's a jealous God. And I kind of like that about Him.

What is an idol, anyway? Simply put, an idol is anything or anyone we serve or love more than we love God.

You might say, "Oh, then I'm golden. I don't serve or love anyone or anything more than God." But let me ask you this: Is there a goal, dream, or desire that you have put all conviction aside to pursue? Is there a relationship that you've stayed in even though you knew it was sinful? Is there something you turn to when you're in need before you turn to God? Do you trust in a plastic god (your credit card) more than God?

Those, my friends, would be idols.

This world *loves* idols. Idolizing money, people, cars, and clout are basically the building blocks of our culture. Especially when it comes to TV and social media. If we plan to break the deeply worldly pattern of idolization, we must first identify the idols in our lives.

RESPOND

1. What do you think God means by saying He is a "jealous" God?

2. We know from the story of Scripture—from creation to the cross to the church—that God would do anything for His children. What are the results of idol worship in the lives of His children? Do these examples help you understand why God chose the word "jealous" to describe Himself?

   When you hear the word "idol," what do you think of?

3. What are some things or people our world idolizes? What is it about those things or people that our world finds so attractive?

ACTIVITY

Let's identify some idols or potential idols in your life.

1. What do you worry about the most? Is it a person? A potential event?

  _____

  _____

  _____

2. How do you spend your money? In particular, the money you have left over after paying bills? What or who are you willing to go into debt for?

  _____

  _____

  _____

3. Who are your most important relationships with? Are there any that pull you away from God?

  _____

  _____

  _____

4. How do you spend your time? Are there mindless activities you turn to more often than productive activities? Do you spend more time at work than you have to? Do you often wish you were somewhere other than the places your responsibilities call you to be?

  _____

  _____

  _____

Not everything you listed above is necessarily an idol. These questions are simply meant to uncover the desires of your heart and direct you to any potential idols.

CHALLENGE

The journey to achieving and maintaining godly grit will often bring us to a place of discomfort. Identifying the idols in our lives will do just that. Looking at the lists you made above, choose at least one that needs to be addressed in your life. Spend some time in prayer confessing that you've either created an idol or are on the brink of idolatry. Then, commit to doing the work to reprioritize so that idolatry is one pattern of the world you do not conform to.

DAY 5

New Rebellion—Unless I Wash You

PAUSE

Take your hand and place it on your heart. Before you dive into the Word, take an emotional temperature. Where is your heart? If it feels pressured, panicked, pursuing other things, ask God to still your heart.

THE PLAN

▶ Prepare to spend at least _____ minutes total in prayer, reading Scripture, and personal study.

▶ Make the link between conformity to this world and pride (even pride in my spiritual life).

▶ Begin a plan.

READ

John 13:3–8:

> ³ *Jesus knew that the Father had put all things under his power, and that he had come from God and was returning to God;* ⁴ *so he got up from the meal, took off his outer clothing, and wrapped a towel around his waist.* ⁵ *After that, he poured water into a basin and began to wash his disciples' feet, drying them with the towel that was wrapped around him.*
>
> ⁶ *He came to Simon Peter, who said to him, "Lord, are you going to wash my feet?"*
>
> ⁷ *Jesus replied, "You do not realize now what I am doing, but later you will understand."*
>
> ⁸ *"No," said Peter, "you shall never wash my feet."*
>
> *Jesus answered, "Unless I wash you, you have no part with me."*

WRITE

In your own handwriting, write out John 13:5.

_____

_____

_____

In this passage, Jesus sets a beautiful example for us of what true humility looks like.

Now, if I had been Peter, I'd have had the same reaction. "No way, Jesus. Get up off those knees. There will be no washing of my feet today! I am unworthy!"

That's the tricky thing about pride. Often, it can come off as insecurity. Pride can also look like unforgiveness, the desire to control, greed, comparison, and jealousy.

Pride is one of the world's most popular patterns. Pride is basically the brand of our culture. Pride also keeps us from being able to renew our minds, because pride focuses all the attention on one person: me.

If you've ever accidentally opened the camera on your phone to a front-facing selfie, you know how ugly an up-close-and-personal image of yourself can look. That's what pride looks like, but in our hearts. It turns us into a me-monster that can't see past ourselves to be thankful for what God has done for us. Pride has certainly come before many of my own falls.

How do we fight against pride? We take a cue from Jesus—by showing deep humility, counting others as more important than ourselves.

RESPOND

1. In the reading, Jesus communicates to Peter about the feet washing three times—what did Jesus have to do to finally get Peter to relent? How did Peter's pride affect his heart?

2. Is there a type of pride that's good? What's the difference between "good" pride and harmful pride?

3. Would you consider yourself a prideful person? Why or why not?

4. What are the dangers of conforming to the pattern of being prideful? Has being prideful ever cost you something? A missed opportunity? The respect of people you care about? Has pride ever created a rift in one of your relationships?

ACTIVITY

Do you know someone who is truly humble? Describe them.

What is it like to be around them?

_____

_____

_____

What habits do they possess?

_____

_____

_____

How do they speak to others?

_____

_____

_____

How do they carry themselves?

_____

_____

_____

What does it feel like to be around them?

_____

_____

_____

CHALLENGE

Find one way to mirror Jesus' humility this week. Study Jesus' actions. Pray and ask God to renew your mind to prepare you to count others as better than yourself.

REFLECTION

Before you begin the next session, spend a few moments reflecting on what you've learned in Session Three.

Reflect on:

How have I grown spiritually—what new patterns am I seeing in my life?

_____

_____

_____

_____

What new ideas about nonconformity have I embraced?

_____

_____

_____

Which Scripture passage is lingering in my mind, and why is it meaningful to me?

_____

_____

_____

_____

How does surrender to God and attentiveness to the Holy Spirit help me take this third step of grit (nonconformity)?

What have I learned about the new rebellion of nonconformity?

What is one thing I *cannot* forget that I learned during this session?

SESSION
GOAL

Consider a different
knee-jerk response

to my suffering—
a response that
doesn't start with
"Why?"

Session 4

THE WHO

STEP FOUR
Lean into the "who" when you wanna ask "why."

SUGGESTED READING
Chapters 8, 9, 10, and 11 of *Grit Don't Quit*

In moments of despair, depression, and disillusion-ment, we need to take a cue from our brother Paul and shake it off. Literally, Paul shook the snake off him and didn't suffer any effects from what should have been a lethal bite.

—*GRIT DON'T QUIT*, PAGE 151

> " Last night an angel of the God to whom I belong and whom I serve stood beside me and said, 'Do not be afraid, Paul. You must stand trial before Caesar; and God has graciously given you the lives of all who sail with you.' So keep up your courage, men, for I have faith in God that it will happen just as he told me. "
>
> —ACTS 27:23–25

WATCH THE SESSION FOUR VIDEO
(stream video or use DVD)

VIDEO OUTLINE QUESTIONS

As you watch the Session Four video, please follow along with the outline. It is meant to help you stay engaged, spark thoughts or questions, and to point out the prevailing themes in each session. As you watch, I encourage you to also take notes or write down points you'd like to follow up on.

▶ Have you spent a lot of your life wondering, *When is it my turn? Why am I the only one who doesn't get what they want? Why is my life so much harder than everyone else's?*

▶ In Acts 27:9–11 Paul said, "Much time had been lost, and sailing had already become dangerous because by now it was after the Day of Atonement. So Paul warned them, 'Men, I can see that our voyage is going to be disastrous and bring great loss to ship and cargo, and to our own lives also.' But the centurion, instead of listening to what Paul said, followed the advice of the pilot and of the owner of the ship." How would you have responded to the centurion ignoring your warning?

▶ Paul was all grit and no gripe: "I have faith that it will happen, just as he told me."

▶ I don't know why, but I do know *Who*.

▶ Like Paul, have you ever encountered God in a moment of darkness?

▶ Sometimes showing grit is about keeping our eyes on heavenly things—
the grittiest thing to do is _____ .

▶ What is your "Malta"? What "Maltas" have you seen others go through?

DISCUSSION QUESTIONS

Friends, let's dig into Bianca's teaching. This is an opportunity to grow together and to get honest! If those words terrify you, that's OK. Take a deep breath and remember that you're going to *get* what you *give* in this study. For us to experience life change, we need to be real about where we are in our lives.

Use these questions as a guide for group conversation. Make sure to leave enough time at the end to share prayer requests and spend a few minutes in prayer.

Conversation Starter: What's the biggest mess you've had to clean up that someone else caused?

1. Paul's story in Acts 27 and 28 is totally wild—let's open our Bibles and recap it together. This is a long one, so consider splitting into four groups. Using the headings, split Paul's journey into four parts: Paul Sails for Rome (27:1–12), The Storm, (27:13–26), The Shipwreck (27:27–44), Paul Ashore on Malta (28:1–10), and assign each group one section.

2. Write bullets of what happened in your section of the story, and share with the group the grit response that Paul showed in your section that stood out to you most.

3. Look up Colossians 3:1–4. According to Paul, why are we able to set our hearts on "things above"? Where does the grit of looking to the "Who" instead of asking "why" lead us—what are we promised?

4. Paul spoke the truth and acknowledged the difficulties that he was facing, but he avoided bitterness. How did he manage this? What kinds of actions did he take?

5. Who or what do you lean into when you want to ask why? Has that been effective? What have been the results of that habit?

6. What would it look like to show grit and set your eyes and hearts on the things above? What would that look like when things are going well? What would that look like when things aren't going well?

7. Have you ever visited "Malta"—a place you never planned on being? How did it feel to be there? What did you do?

8. How are you at "shaking it off"? What does "shaking it off" look like in your life? How could you become a person who is able to shake it off in moments of despair, depression, and disillusionment?

Before Next Time: We're going to wrap up this discussion with a few reminders about the next meeting and about the personal study.

Our next meeting, time and place:

In this week's personal study, we'll leave behind "Why?" for "Who" through Scripture, prayer, and study.

What I'm hoping to get out of the personal study.

Leader Note: Close out the session by asking if anyone has a specific prayer request to share with the group. Then, lead the group in a prayer to close. If you feel led, you can also ask someone else in the group to lead the closing prayer. Feel free to use the prayer below to get started.

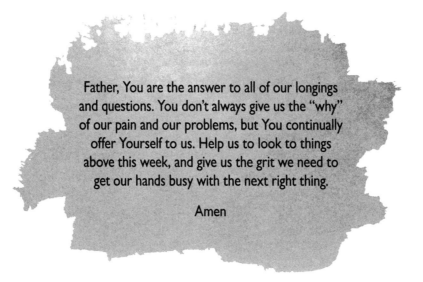

Father, You are the answer to all of our longings and questions. You don't always give us the "why" of our pain and our problems, but You continually offer Yourself to us. Help us to look to things above this week, and give us the grit we need to get our hands busy with the next right thing.

Amen

Session 4

THE
WHO

PERSONAL
STUDY
Getting Gritty

Participants are to complete the following questions at home, ideally over the course of five different days. **If there are any questions you did not get to during the Group Discussion, I encourage you to work through those during the at-home study time.**

> "Paul learned what we have to learn too: when you make it through the storm and all hell breaks loose on the shore—when you've been through all and it still keeps coming—we've got to make like Paul and *shake! it! off!*"

—GRIT DON'T QUIT, PAGE 151

DAY I

The Who—Are You the One?

PAUSE

Before we start this week of homework, take fifteen seconds to ask God to speak to you in ways only He can.

THE PLAN

▶ Prepare to spend at least _____ minutes total in prayer, reading Scripture, and personal study.

▶ Articulate some of my expectations about the way God is supposed to act, and to move toward "Who" instead of "Why?"

▶ Begin a plan.

READ

Matthew 11:2–6:

> ² *When John, who was in prison, heard about the deeds of the Messiah, he sent his disciples* ³ *to ask him, "Are you the one who is to come, or should we expect someone else?"*
>
> ⁴ *Jesus replied, "Go back and report to John what you hear and see:* ⁵ *The blind receive sight, the lame walk, those who have leprosy are cleansed, the deaf hear, the dead are raised, and the good news is proclaimed to the poor.* ⁶ *Blessed is anyone who does not stumble on account of me."*

WRITE

In your own handwriting, write out Matthew 11:5.

_____

_____

If you've learned how to be a person who moves through life without any expectations for how it'll go, I want to know your secret. I'm serious! I have ideas, hopes, and visions for what each day and even the future will hold for me, my family, and my career. Can you relate?

And when life *doesn't* meet our expectations, it can sting. In fact, depending on the level of disappointment, unmet expectations can deeply wound us—send us reeling. Cause us trauma. Sometimes, they can even make us question God.

Believe it or not, John the Baptist himself had this very experience. John was in prison for criticizing Herod's relationship choices. We're not exactly sure *what* unmet expectations John was experiencing, but it's safe to assume that since he was in jail . . . he expected to get out. He was waiting on Jesus to come to his rescue. John essentially says, "Are you the Messiah or not? If you are, why am I still in here? Is there someone with some actual power we should be expecting?"

Have you ever been where John was? In a prison of pain? A prison of uncertainty? A prison of doubt? A prison of unmet expectations? If that's you right now, listen to Jesus' response:

"Go back and report to John what you hear and see." Then Jesus lists all the miracles and works He'd been performing. Then He says, "Blessed is anyone who does not stumble on account of me."

In essence, Jesus is telling John that the gritty thing to do in the face of unmet expectations is to think about all I've done. Remember all I still do. Those who can remain certain of God's power and love, even when the timing seems off and the plan all wrong, will be blessed.

RESPOND

1. Look up Isaiah 35:3–6. What does the connection between these words of prophecy (and others like it—feel free to look up more of them in a Bible app or just on a plain old Google search!) and Jesus' assertion to John reveal about God's perspective on time?

2. How does it make you feel when God doesn't meet your expectations? How do you usually react when your expectations aren't met? Does your reaction change the outcome?

3. Are you in a "prison" of your own right now? How are you talking to God about where you are and how you feel? What would it look like for God to release you from that prison?

ACTIVITY

Miracles don't have to involve the multiplication of food or the raising of the dead—a miracle is a sign of God's presence and power. Miracles come in all shapes and sizes. Can you think of anything that's happened to you—a restored relationship, a physical healing, a met need—that you'd consider a miracle? List any of these below.

_____   _____

_____   _____

_____   _____

CHALLENGE

In light of all the miracles you've witnessed or heard of, how can you shift your perspective in moments of unmet expectations? Spend a few minutes journaling your response. This change of perspective doesn't mean we can't ask for what we need, though. We just need to focus on "Who" instead of "Why?"—this shift helps us recognize miracles in the first place. In boldness, take a moment to ask God for a miracle.

DAY 2

The Who—The Lord is Good

PAUSE

Before diving into God's Word, pause and state one thing you are grateful to God for.

THE PLAN

▶ Prepare to spend at least _____ minutes total in prayer, reading Scripture, and personal study.

▶ Consider whether or not I'd use the word "good" to describe God.

▶ Begin a plan.

READ

Psalm 34:8:

> *Taste and see that the LORD is good; blessed is the one who takes refuge in him.*

John 10:11:

> **11** *"I am the good shepherd. The good shepherd lays down his life for the sheep.*

I Chronicles 16:24:

> **24** *Declare his glory among the nations, his marvelous deeds among all peoples.*

Mark 10:18:

> **18** *"Why do you call me good?" Jesus answered. "No one is good—except God alone."*

WRITE

In your own handwriting, write out Psalm 34:8.

_____

_____

God often gets described as "good." You've heard it before—"Our God is good!"; "God is so good to me!" And Jesus says it Himself—God alone could be described as "good."

But sometimes it doesn't *feel* like He's that good. Yeah, we can go there. People of faith have been asking this question forever:

RESPOND

1. What do you think it means to "take refuge" in God?

2. What does "declaring God's glory" look like throughout history? You don't have to do a whole research project, just sketch out a few ideas that come to mind right now. Think of the Old Testament Israelites, the first Christians, Christians throughout history, and us today. How are some of the ways we declare His glory similar to those who came before us? What has changed?

3. We are tempted to judge God based on a few painful stories or circumstances. How would you feel if that's how others judged you?

4. Can you be healed without having all of the answers to your questions? Why or why not? What does healing look like?

ACTIVITY

Do you believe God is good? Do your actions, prayer life, words, thoughts, and habits reflect that belief? List some of your habits. For example, commitment to a daily prayer time, or a tendency to get angry when things don't go according to plan (yep—we're talking good and bad habits). Reflect on what these habits reveal about your beliefs about God's character. Do you believe He is good? Do you trust Him?

CHALLENGE

God is good because He *is* goodness. He doesn't ever change—His character is not altered by our circumstances. And yet—He cares about what happens to you. Take a moment to think about one of the difficult circumstances you're facing right now. What feelings arise in your heart when you ask, "Why?" Does your perspective on the circumstance shift when you think about "Who" instead?

DAY 3

The Who—And It Was Very Good

PAUSE

Close your eyes and count to ten slowly. Calm your mind before starting today's reading.

THE PLAN

▷ Prepare to spend at least _____ minutes total in prayer, reading Scripture, and personal study.

▷ Read the story of creation, and take a moment to contemplate the goodness of what God did.

▷ Begin a plan.

READ

Genesis 1:1–31:

> ¹ *In the beginning God created the heavens and the earth.* ² *Now the earth was formless and empty, darkness was over the surface of the deep, and the Spirit of God was hovering over the waters.*
>
> ³ *And God said, "Let there be light," and there was light.* ⁴ *God saw that the light was good, and he separated the light from the darkness.* ⁵ *God called the light "day," and the darkness he called "night." And there was evening, and there was morning—the first day.*
>
> ⁶ *And God said, "Let there be a vault between the waters to separate water from water."* ⁷ *So God made the vault and separated the water under the vault from the water above it. And it was so.* ⁸ *God called the vault "sky." And there was evening, and there was morning—the second day.*
>
> ⁹ *And God said, "Let the water under the sky be gathered to one place, and let dry ground appear." And it was so.* ¹⁰ *God called the dry ground "land," and the gathered waters he called "seas." And God saw that it was good.*

[11] Then God said, "Let the land produce vegetation: seed-bearing plants and trees on the land that bear fruit with seed in it, according to their various kinds." And it was so. [12] The land produced vegetation: plants bearing seed according to their kinds and trees bearing fruit with seed in it according to their kinds. And God saw that it was good. [13] And there was evening, and there was morning—the third day.

[14] And God said, "Let there be lights in the vault of the sky to separate the day from the night, and let them serve as signs to mark sacred times, and days and years, [15] and let them be lights in the vault of the sky to give light on the earth." And it was so. [16] God made two great lights—the greater light to govern the day and the lesser light to govern the night. He also made the stars. [17] God set them in the vault of the sky to give light on the earth, [18] to govern the day and the night, and to separate light from darkness. And God saw that it was good. [19] And there was evening, and there was morning—the fourth day.

[20] And God said, "Let the water teem with living creatures, and let birds fly above the earth across the vault of the sky." [21] So God created the great creatures of the sea and every living thing with which the water teems and that moves about in it, according to their kinds, and every winged bird according to its kind. And God saw that it was good. [22] God blessed them and said, "Be fruitful and increase in number and fill the water in the seas, and let the birds increase on the earth." [23] And there was evening, and there was morning—the fifth day.

[24] And God said, "Let the land produce living creatures according to their kinds: the livestock, the creatures that move along the ground, and the wild animals, each according to its kind." And it was so. [25] God made the wild animals according to their kinds, the livestock according to their kinds, and all the creatures that move along the ground according to their kinds. And God saw that it was good.

[26] Then God said, "Let us make mankind in our image, in our likeness, so that they may rule over the fish in the sea and the birds in the sky, over the livestock and all the wild animals,[a] and over all the creatures that move along the ground."

[27] So God created mankind in his own image, in the image of God he created them; male and female he created them.

28 *God blessed them and said to them, "Be fruitful and increase in number; fill the earth and subdue it. Rule over the fish in the sea and the birds in the sky and over every living creature that moves on the ground."*

29 *Then God said, "I give you every seed-bearing plant on the face of the whole earth and every tree that has fruit with seed in it. They will be yours for food.* **30** *And to all the beasts of the earth and all the birds in the sky and all the creatures that move along the ground—everything that has the breath of life in it—I give every green plant for food." And it was so.*

31 *God saw all that he had made, and it was very good.*

WRITE

In your own handwriting, write out Genesis 1:31.

Picture it. The laundry has been washed, dried, *and even put away.* The sink is empty, the dishes are in the dishwasher, which is humming along pleasantly in the background. The counters are *not*, in fact, covered in unidentifiable stickiness and crumbs. You look around. Even your throw blankets strike that perfect folded-but-not-folded vibe that's almost impossible without the help of a design expert.

Your house isn't just clean. Your house is *good.*

But then what happens? Eventually, it gets un-good. Your friends come over and leave dishes to be washed. The dog chews up another down-filled pillow. And your roommate or husband has the *nerve* to use your throw blanket as an actual blanket. It's a tale as old as time, isn't it? And it's one God is familiar with, but on a whole other level.

When God created our universe, He created it *good.* He even created Adam and Eve to be *good.* There was no sin. There was no shame. There was no pain. But what did exist was free will. And even *that* choice to choose to obey God or not is further proof of God's goodness. Unfortunately, Adam and Eve chose wrong. They chose to sin, ushering in a world of hurt for themselves, and as their ancestors, for us as well.

In that very moment of choice—in that moment of sin—humans came into God's good, clean house and made a giant mess of it. But also in that moment, our redemption story began.

In times when we want to ask why, we can remember that this world is not our permanent residence. We have a sparkling, gleaming forever-home awaiting us in heaven. A home headed by our good Father, who is still willing to clean up after us, even today.

RESPOND

1. Read verse 26 again—what word does God use to refer to Himself? How are we different than the rest of His creation? What understandings can we have about His goodness because of this difference?

2. Have you ever made a mess of something that didn't belong to you? You stained the shirt you borrowed? You rear-ended someone else's car? You fumbled the client meeting and lost the deal for your business? How did you feel? What did you do?

3. In the moments we feel disappointed, challenged, or in pain, why is it tempting for us to blame or question God? Does blaming God bring us healing? Explain your response.

Activity

When you think about the world today, what adjectives would you use to describe it? Make a list below.

Did you use the term "good"? Why or why not?

Write a prayer to God in your journal. Ask Him to reveal the goodness that is still very much in the world. Then, ask Him to help you contribute to that good.

CHALLENGE

If you can go outside, spend a few minutes taking a walk. If you can't, find a window! Take in all that God created for you. Look for the beauty in His creation. It may no longer be wholly good, but you can be sure it is wholly redeemed.

DAY 4

The Who—Co-Heirs with Christ

PAUSE

Take three long breaths by inhaling for four seconds, holding for four seconds, exhaling for four seconds. Repeat three times.

THE PLAN

▶ Prepare to spend at least _____ minutes total in prayer, reading Scripture, and personal study.

▶ Through reading Paul's words, renew my perspective on suffering.

▶ Begin a plan.

READ

Romans 8:17–21:

> [17] *Now if we are children, then we are heirs—heirs of God and co-heirs with Christ, if indeed we share in his sufferings in order that we may also share in his glory.*
>
> [18] *I consider that our present sufferings are not worth comparing with the glory that will be revealed in us.* [19] *For the creation waits in eager expectation for the children of God to be revealed.* [20] *For the creation was subjected to frustration, not by its own choice, but by the will of the one who subjected it, in hope* [21] *that the creation itself will be liberated from its bondage to decay and brought into the freedom and glory of the children of God.*

WRITE

In your own handwriting, write out Romans 8:18.

Why didn't God heal my mother?

Why didn't God save my marriage?

Why won't God give us a baby?

Why won't God bring me a spouse?

Why did God allow that betrayal?

In ministry, I get asked a lot of tough questions about God. The truth is, in moments where my grit has faltered, I've asked some of these questions myself. All God would have to do is lead someone to the cure for cancer. All He'd have to do is move one geological plate to eradicate hurricanes and tsunamis. What we're really saying is that we want God to make things better right now so that things will be easier for us right now.

If God is all-powerful, all-knowing, and all-good, why doesn't he make things better *right now?*

Paul tells us. First, he tells us that if we want to share in the inheritance of Christ (forgiveness, salvation, heaven), we have to share in the suffering of Christ. I think we often forget that Jesus, though fully God, was also fully man. And during His time on earth, He experienced great suffering. He was persecuted by the religious leaders of His day; He was mocked and teased; He was under great suspicion and constant questions; He was tempted by the devil; He experienced great sorrow . . . and we haven't even made it to the cross.

If Jesus Himself suffered on earth, what makes us think that we shouldn't suffer too?

But Paul also leaves us with hope. Our sufferings here on earth are *nothing* compared to the glory that lies ahead. And, one day, creation "will be liberated from its bondage to decay and brought into the freedom and glory of the children of God."

RESPOND

1. We are, with Christ, God's "heirs." According to Paul, what is our two-part inheritance?

2. Explain the word "suffering" in your own words. Have you ever experienced physical suffering? Emotional? Describe what that felt like?

3. Can you think of any good aspects of an inheritance of suffering? For example, has suffering shaped your character—made you more empathetic, or honest, or gritty? Use a sentence or two to explain.

4. Is it difficult for you to picture Jesus as a human? Is it easier for you to believe that He ascended into heaven than it is for you to believe that His heart ached when He learned of Lazarus' death? Why do you think it's easier to embrace Jesus-as-God than it is for you to embrace Jesus-as-man?

ACTIVITY

Read the following and record the ways in which He suffered.

John 11 _____

Matthew 26 _____

John 5:1–28 _____

What surprises you about what you read? How can Jesus' reactions inform our own reactions to suffering?

CHALLENGE

This week, whenever you feel tempted to question God, be intentional to pause and think, *Did Jesus go through something like this? Or something worse?*

I'm not trying to minimize your pain. It's completely acceptable to hurt, grieve, and even to be angry. But contextualizing your pain reminds us that we are not alone. Jesus has been right where we are. And He has promised to walk alongside us on our own paths through pain.

DAY 5

The Who—He Who Promised Is Faithful

PAUSE

Take your hand and place it on your heart. Before you dive into the Word, take an emotional temperature. Where is your heart? If it feels pressured, panicked, pursuing other things, ask God to still your heart.

THE PLAN

▶ Prepare to spend at least _____ minutes total in prayer, reading Scripture, and personal study.

▶ Ponder God's faithfulness and its practical applications for my life.

▶ Begin a plan.

READ

Hebrews 10:23–25:

> **23** *Let us hold unswervingly to the hope we profess, for he who promised is faithful.* **24** *And let us consider how we may spur one another on toward love and good deeds,* **25** *not giving up meeting together, as some are in the habit of doing, but encouraging one another—and all the more as you see the Day approaching.*

WRITE

In your own handwriting, write out Hebrews 10:23.

When we are in seasons of suffering, it can be our tendency to isolate ourselves. Or is that just me?

Maybe we're embarrassed that we're still in pain. Maybe we tell ourselves we should be over "it" by now. Or that our grief is a sign of weakness. Or that no one can understand how we're feeling, so it's better to just keep our pain to ourselves. Instead of being vulnerable, we stuff our feelings and thoughts deep down into the trenches of our hearts.

But that's not how God wants us to live. He wants us to be connected to one another—to other believers—to share our lives together. And not just the gussied-up good stuff in our lives, but the I-could-never-speak-this-thing-out-loud stuff too. That's why Jesus established the church.

The Bible refers to the church as the body of Christ. In a letter to the Corinthians, Paul says every member plays a part. "If one part suffers, every part suffers with it; if one part is honored, every part rejoices with it" (1 Corinthians 12:26).

Yes, God wants us to share in one another's sufferings. This might be a challenge for you if you're a particularly guarded person. You may even have some very real reasons to be guarded! But Jesus has called us to something *better.* A respite by-way-of His people. If you aren't in a faith community right now, you are missing out on God's provision for your pain. He wants you connected to people who love and follow Him so you can help *each other* love and follow Him, especially during seasons when you want to ask why.

ACTIVITY

1. Read Hebrews 10:23–25 again—list out a few things that happen in healthy faith communities.

----

2. Is it difficult for you to be vulnerable with others? Why or why not?

_____

_____

_____

3. How did Jesus model vulnerability during His life and ministry? What can we learn from Jesus' decision to establish disciples and the church itself?

_____

_____

_____

4. How would your life look if you decided to commit yourself to a faith community and were honest about your suffering and pain? In what ways would you be taking a risk? Do you think it would benefit your life?

_____

_____

_____

CHALLENGE

Find a way to be vulnerable with someone this week. Maybe it's a text that says, "You know how I told you I was doing OK? Well, I'm not." Maybe it's a prayer to God where you finally confess your doubt, anger, or grief. Maybe it's being more honest during group time next week!

When we invite God's people into our suffering, we invite _God_ into our suffering—the only _Who_ who can heal us.

REFLECTION

Before you begin the next session, spend a few moments reflecting on what you've learned in Session Four.

Reflect on:

How have I grown spiritually—have I been consistent with small changes?

_____

_____

_____

How has my perspective on suffering changed over the past week?

_____

_____

_____

What new ideas have I embraced?

_____

_____

_____

What have I learned about leaning into the Who when I wanna ask why?

_____

_____

_____

Can I see God's goodness even in that one bad situation—the one that keeps coming up?

_____

_____

_____

What is one thing I *cannot* forget that I learned during this session?

_____

SESSION GOAL

Leave this study with my eyes on the prize, encouraged by

His word, and equipped with strategies for staying gritty for the long haul.

Session 5

STRAIGHTEN YOUR CROWN

STEP FIVE

Keep your eye on the prize—a crown that lasts forever.

SUGGESTED READING

Finish *Grit Don't Quit*

"With every step closer to your purpose, with every sacrifice endured, with every promise from God that you hold on to, with every trial you survive, you are adding to the foundation of faith for the next generation to stand upon. The ripple effect of your life will reach future generations—for good or for bad, whether you want it to or not. You are making a mark one way or another, so the question is, *What mark will you leave?*"

—*GRIT DON'T QUIT*, PAGES 192–93

> **"** Do you not know that in a race all the runners run, but only one gets the prize? Run in such a way as to get the prize. Everyone who competes in the games goes into strict training. They do it to get a crown that will not last, but we do it to get a crown that will last forever. **"**
>
> ### 1 CORINTHIANS 9:24–25

INTRODUCTION

Today, we place crowns on the heads of athletes, pageant winners, monarchs, and women celebrating their "Dirty Thirty" birthdays. Crowns today are used as a symbol of significance, honor, and pride. But do you know what ancient headgear inspired the crown?

Helmets.

Helmets! *I know!* In Classical times, the chief of a barbarian tribe often wore a distinctive helmet that set him apart from his followers. I love that! And I think that if we viewed our spiritual crowns more like helmets, it would shift our perspective. It would clarify how to maintain grit over the long haul. It would create a more accurate mental picture for the battle that lies ahead.

Because, friends, while we may be daughters of a king, we are more than dainty, crown-wearing princesses waiting to be rescued. Instead, we are soldiers who are locked and loaded to face our foe in the race of life that Christ has set before us. We have access to the armor of God (Ephesians 6:10–18) and there is no competitor who can best us if we choose the godly grit offered to us through His Holy Spirit.

And, yes, there is strict training involved in this race. But we have the master coach in our hearts and by our sides. So, when I tell you to straighten your crown, here's what I mean: Remember that by the power of God, His

Holy Spirit, and the steadfastness of your godly grit, you are more than a conqueror through Christ.

WATCH THE SESSION FIVE VIDEO
(stream video or use DVD)

VIDEO OUTLINE QUESTIONS

As you watch the Session Five video, please follow along with the outline. It is meant to help you stay engaged, spark thoughts or questions, and to point out the prevailing themes in each session. As you watch, I encourage you to also take notes or write down points you'd like to follow up on.

▶ When you think of a crown, who do you picture wearing it?

▶ What's your reaction to Paul saying that in order to "compete in the game" you must endure strict training?

▶ When you look back at your most discouraging moments, do you remember being isolated or with a community?

▶ When we wanna quit, worship gives us _____ .

▶ How might your life be different if you embraced that you are "more than a conqueror" through Christ?

▶ What's our source of grit?

DISCUSSION QUESTIONS

Friends, let's dig into Bianca's teaching. This is an opportunity to grow together and to get honest!! If those words terrify you, that's OK. Take a deep breath and remember that you're going to *get* what you *give* in this study. For us to experience life change, we need to be real about where we are in our lives. Use these questions as a guide for group conversation. Make sure to leave enough time at the end to share prayer requests and spend a few minutes in prayer.

Conversation Starter: Have you ever entered a race or competed for a prize?

1. We've read some incredible Paul stories together. Were any of them completely new to you? Do you have a favorite "grit moment" from your new favorite, the one and only Apostle Paul?

2. Read 1 Corinthians 9:25–27 again. In matters of faith, what does "training" look like? What kinds of things (maybe actions or attitudes) would merit a "disqualification" in the race of faith?

3. Paul and Silas brought the house down—quite literally—during their stay in prison (Acts 16:16–34, if you want to reference). How did the effects of Paul's and Silas's actions ripple out to the others around them? How did God use their suffering for His glory?

4. Bianca taught about Paul's defense in Romans 8:31–38. Read the passage again. We're running in a race that is already won—even though we've failed before and will probably fail again, we are already conquerers. How does this knowledge shift your perspective about the race of faith—about training, about finishing, and about showing grit along the way?

5. When's the last time that you quit something before you were finished? What did you quit? How did you feel after?

6. What "prizes" does our world mistakenly run after? What "prizes" have you mistakenly run after?

7. We're not expected to be perfect. (Maybe read that again!) We're going to trip over the hurdles of life. Have you ever "tripped" over one of life's hurdles? Share about that experience.

8. Paul and Silas were singing hymns to God at midnight. In the "midnight" of your own suffering, how do you usually respond? How might singing hymns to God change the outcome?

9. Do you have "gritty" people surrounding your life? If you don't, what can you do this week to change that?

10. As the last group session comes to a close, is there anything you want to share about your experience in this study? What is one thing you learned that you don't want to forget?

Last Group Meeting! We're going to wrap up this final discussion with a few reminders about the personal study.

This session was Bianca's final teaching. Thank each other for the time and the grit that you all put into this study together!

In this week's personal study, we'll find inspiration for grit in the everyday— how we apply what we've been taught even after this study is over.

What I'm hoping to take with me from this study:

_____

_____

_____

Leader Note: Close out the session by asking if anyone has a specific prayer request to share with the group. Then, lead the group in a prayer to close. If you feel led, you can also ask someone else in the group to lead the closing prayer. Feel free to use this prayer to get you started.

Father, we want to praise You in every prison we ever find ourselves in. We want to run the race to win the prize, because You've already made us more than conquerors. You are the ultimate example of grit—You've never given up on Your children. You've crowned us with Your victory and You offer us Your grit. Help us to run flat out for that prize.

Amen

Session 5

STRAIGHTEN YOUR CROWN

PERSONAL STUDY
Getting Gritty

Complete these final questions and activities on your own this week. **If there are any remaining questions or thoughts sparked from your personal study, I encourage you to reach out to your group leader or a member of your group and continue the conversation and journey following Paul's example and living a life known by your grit!**

"When we look at Paul's life holistically, we see that the sacrifice was a daily activity. He gave up what most people would boast in—his education, his pedigree, his social clout—and didn't stop there. Paul told the Philippians that his background, his religious heritage, and his accomplishments were counted as "loss." And he didn't stop there. He told his friends in Philippi, "What is more, I consider everything a loss because of the surpassing worth of knowing Christ Jesus my Lord, for whose sake I have lost all things. I consider them garbage, that I may gain Christ" (Philippians 3:8). Instead of leveraging his pedigree or boasting in education, Paul poured every last drop out for the gospel, for the church, and for the Lord. His life after meeting Jesus on the Damascus Road was a drink offering to the Lord."

—*GRIT DON'T QUIT*, PAGE 198

DAY 1

Straighten Your Crown—For Such a Time as This

PAUSE

Before we start this final week of homework, take fifteen seconds to ask God to speak to you in ways only He can.

THE PLAN

▶ Spend at least _____ minutes total in prayer, reading Scripture, and personal study.

▶ Find some inspiration in the story of Esther.

▶ Begin a plan.

READ

Esther 4:12–16:

> ¹² When Esther's words were reported to Mordecai, ¹³ he sent back this answer: "Do not think that because you are in the king's house you alone of all the Jews will escape. ¹⁴ For if you remain silent at this time, relief and deliverance for the Jews will arise from another place, but you and your father's family will perish. And who knows but that you have come to your royal position for such a time as this?"

> ¹⁵ Then Esther sent this reply to Mordecai: ¹⁶ "Go, gather together all the Jews who are in Susa, and fast for me. Do not eat or drink for three days, night or day. I and my attendants will fast as you do. When this is done, I will go to the king, even though it is against the law. And if I perish, I perish."

WRITE

In your own handwriting, write out Esther 4:14.

_____

_____

_____

_____

Esther is one of my favorite characters in the Bible. Not only did she have an actual crown as King Xerxes' queen, but she had a let's-do-this-thing, gritty attitude that we could all learn from.

When her cousin Mordecai told Esther about Haman's plot to eradicate the Jews in the entire kingdom, she had a choice to make: Did she risk her life to save her people or did she play it safe and hope someone else intervened? She didn't have long to decide. As you may know, Esther sent word back to Mordecai to gather all the Jews he could to pray and fast for her.

Queen Homegirl was going into battle. And like a line from an action movie come her parting words to him: "And if I die, I die."

I'm not sure of Esther's mental state, but I imagine she was ridden with anxiety. Would King Xerxes hear her request? Would he kill her? Would her entire family and people be murdered? Whatever the outcome, Esther gritted through her very likely concerns to keep her eye on the prize—a crown that would last forever.

RESPOND

1. How did Esther resist isolating herself during this time of anxiety? What did she ask others to do for her? Have you ever asked anyone to do this for you?

2. If you had been Esther, how would you have responded to Mordecai's request? What do you imagine Esther was thinking and feeling during those three days of prayer and fasting?

3. God probably isn't asking you to go before a king and ask that he spare the lives of an entire people. But He may be asking you to do something else—something that would require a risk. Is that true for you in the race of life you're running right now? What risk is God asking you to take?

ACTIVITY

Esther kept her eye on the prize by accepting her fate. She played out the worst-case scenario for herself and knew what was at stake. "If I die, I die." Because Esther knew that some things are worth the risk.

What is your worst first? Your biggest concern? Your greatest worry? Esther said, "If I die, I die." Fill in the blank with your own version of that statement.

Example: "If I never find a husband, I will live my life as a single woman."

"If I _____,

I _____."

Often, we are afraid to put into words what we fear. Now, add this line to the third blank above: "But GOD!"

Esther kept her eye on the prize by focusing on the picture bigger—on the grandest glory. And because of that, the crown she wore on earth was surely a shadow of the crown she wears in heaven.

CHALLENGE

Write "But GOD!" on a sticky note or paper you will see every day. Use that as a reminder that even if your worst fear comes true . . . "But God!"

DAY 2

Straighten Your Crown—Heavenward

PAUSE

Before diving into God's Word, pause and state one thing you are grateful to God for.

THE PLAN

▶ Spend at least _____minutes total in prayer, reading Scripture, and personal study.

▶ Allow myself to leave the past behind, and start fixing my focus on the goal that Paul writes about.

▶ Begin a plan.

READ

Philippians 3:12–14:

> [12] *Not that I have already obtained all this, or have already arrived at my goal, but I press on to take hold of that for which Christ Jesus took hold of me.* [13] *Brothers and sisters, I do not consider myself yet to have taken hold of it. But one thing I do: Forgetting what is behind and straining toward what is ahead,* [14] *I press on toward the goal to win the prize for which God has called me heavenward in Christ Jesus.*

WRITE

In your own handwriting, write out Philippians 3:13.

_____

_____

_____

Paul was aggressive, wasn't he? All this racing and pushing! Maybe that's why I relate to him so much—I can be a little *passionate* as well.

But one of the most important things we learn about grit is found here in Philippians: "Forgetting what is behind and straining toward what is ahead."

When you're watching a baseball game or any type of competition, when an athlete makes an error, they don't get to pause the game in order to go back to the location of the error and redo it. Nope. It's done. It's behind. It's in the past. Sometimes, players can shake it off. (Another Paul-ism!) Sometimes, they can get their head back in the game and finish well.

Others . . . not so much. Other times, players can become rattled by an error. So they make another one. And another. If you've ever watched Major League Baseball, you've probably seen a pitcher or two fall apart on the mound. Or if you've watched a gymnast fall off the balance beam, you've seen him or her remain incredibly shaky for the rest of the routine.

According to Paul, we cannot live life in light of our past. We live our life *straining* forward. I love that word: *straining.* I imagine myself gritting my teeth and leaning all the way forward. Living in the past will do nothing for your future. It will also deplete your grit. Besides, you can't keep your eye on the prize for which God has called you with your eyes on the rearview mirror.

RESPOND

1. Flip over to 1 Corinthians 9:24–27. Paul's using the same idea here as he did for the Philippians. Do you see any differences in these verses? What new understanding does it bring up for you about faith as a "race"?

2. Have you ever made an innocent, public error? You flubbed a word in a presentation, you called someone by the wrong name. How did you feel? How often do you still think about it?

3. Is there a bigger moral failure in your past? (Spoiler alert: We all have moral failures in our past.) How does it feel when you think about that situation? Have you asked God to forgive you? Is your shame from your past holding you back from keeping your eye on the prize? In what ways?

ACTIVITY

In your journal, write a letter to your past self. Speak to her through the Holy Spirit. Tell her God's words about her. And most importantly, release her from the past. Tell her that it's time to strain forward, keeping her eye on the prize.

CHALLENGE

We certainly can't strain forward toward the prize while we're focused on our past. Instead, Paul tells us to set our eyes and hearts on the things above. Make a short list below of all the ways you can intentionally set your eyes and hearts on God this week.

DAY 3

Straigthen Your Crown—Fallen Away from Grace

PAUSE

Close your eyes and count to ten slowly. Calm your mind before starting today's reading.

THE PLAN

▶ Spend at least _____minutes total in prayer, reading Scripture, and personal study.

▶ Understand a few strategies for getting back on track when I lose sight of the prize.

▶ Begin a plan.

READ

Galatians 5:4–9:

> 4 *You who are trying to be justified by the law have been alienated from Christ; you have fallen away from grace.* 5 *For through the Spirit we eagerly await by faith the righteousness for which we hope.* 6 *For in Christ Jesus neither circumcision nor uncircumcision has any value. The only thing that counts is faith expressing itself through love.*
>
> 7 *You were running a good race. Who cut in on you to keep you from obeying the truth?* 8 *That kind of persuasion does not come from the one who calls you.* 9 *"A little yeast works through the whole batch of dough."*

WRITE

In your own handwriting, write out Galatians 5:7.

"If you lay down with dogs, you're gonna get fleas." You may have heard this saying before. Verse 9 above is like it: "A little yeast works through the whole batch of dough." What is Paul saying to the church of Galatia?

First, Paul is ticked. Or, at the very least, exasperated. The Galatians had fallen back into former habits by observing customs under the old law. Paul says, "What the heck happened, guys? You were doing so well! You were running a great race!" Then he asks, "Who cut in on you to keep you from obeying the truth?"

In other words, who is your influence right now? Who changed your course? Who cut in on you to push you backward in the race? Paul noticed what a lot of us as parents and stepparents notice: Who we spend a lot of time with greatly affects our lives—for better or for worse.

RESPOND

1. Paul really has a thing for this race metaphor! What did the Galatians do that pulled them so far off course—check verse 4. What were they trying to do?

2. Have you ever been running a great race in life and had someone "cut in on you," distracting you from the prize ahead? What happened?

3. If we want to run a good race, we've got to have solid teammates. Teammates who encourage us, uplift us, and keep us on track. Who is on your "team" in life right now? How do they keep you on track? Or how might they potentially "cut in on you," distracting you from the prize ahead?

ACTIVITY

This isn't about the blame game—it's about "team" awareness. It's about understanding that a little bit of yeast can work its way through all the dough. Think through the times in your life when you got off track. Write them down in your journal. Now, write down the names of the people who were closest to you during that time.

Do you notice anything significant about your "teammates"? Did this exercise reveal anything about your *current* teammates in life? If so, what?

CHALLENGE

This may be a difficult exercise but think back on your relationships. Have *you* ever been the yeast in someone's otherwise good dough? What would you do differently if you could go back in time? Have you ever reached out and apologized to that person for getting them off track? Consider doing so this week.

DAY 4

Straighten Your Crown—The Point of Death

PAUSE

Take three long breaths by inhaling for four seconds, holding for four seconds, exhaling for four seconds. Repeat three times.

THE PLAN

▶ Spend at least _____minutes total in prayer, reading Scripture, and personal study.

▶ Deepen my understanding of the word "crown" and the way it's used in the Bible.

▶ Begin a plan.

READ

Revelation 2:10:

> [10] *Do not be afraid of what you are about to suffer. I tell you, the devil will put some of you in prison to test you, and you will suffer persecution for ten days. Be faithful, even to the point of death, and I will give you life as your victor's crown.*

WRITE

In your own handwriting, write out Revelation 2:10.

_____

_____

The "victor's crown" is a crown for all believers, especially for those who have endured suffering. Which, by my check, is all of us. But if we can remain faithful and show grit for the long haul, we are promised a crown of life. I don't know about you, but to me, that crown sounds sort of amazing. But what does a "crown of life" mean?

John 10:10 quotes Jesus as saying, "I have come that they may have life, and have it to the full." In other words, we all need physical sustenance to survive this life. Things like food, water, oxygen, and shelter. Jesus came to give us spiritual sustenance. Things like salvation, hope, grace, forgiveness, and joy.

We know that our earthly lives will end, but we have the promise of *real life* awaiting us in heaven: "And this is what he promised us—eternal life" (1 John 2:25).

Keep your eyes on the prize ahead—the eternal life promised to us through Jesus.

RESPOND

1. Suffering is not a "maybe" for any of us. What encouragement does this verse give us about suffering? When we're tempted to worry about what's going to happen to us next, what kind of attitude should we have instead? What are we promised if we are faithful?

2. Is it strange or uncomfortable for you to think about life in heaven? What do you envision heaven to look like or be like? What movies have you seen or books have you read about heaven? Do you think those are accurate? What do you hope heaven is like?

3. Do you live as if you're wearing a crown of life? Do you value the eternal over the temporal? How might you shift your focus and priorities to wear the crown of life?

ACTIVITY

When we look at where we spend the most time and money, there we can find what we value most in life. Make a list below of what your *actions* show to be your priorities when it comes to time and money.

TIME	MONEY

Looking at your list. Is it accurate to say that you are wearing the crown of life? That you prioritize eternal things over the things of this world? If not, what things need to leave your life?

CHALLENGE

Make a shift in your priorities this week. Move at least one item off the list you made above that doesn't prioritize the eternal.

DAY 5

Straighten Your Crown—Is It Not You?

PAUSE

Take your hand and place it on your heart. Before you dive into the Word, take an emotional temperature. Where is your heart? If it feels pressured, panicked, pursuing other things, ask God to still your heart.

THE PLAN

▶ Spend at least _____minutes total in prayer, reading Scripture, and personal study.

▶ Consider how I've grown in grit over the past few weeks.

▶ Begin a plan.

READ

1 Thessalonians 2:19–20:

> **19** *For what is our hope, our joy, or the crown in which we will glory in the presence of our Lord Jesus when he comes? Is it not you?* **20** *Indeed, you are our glory and joy.*

WRITE

In your own handwriting, write out 1 Thessalonians 2:19–20.

_____

_____

_____

_____

The world has its way of taking holy things and creating its own counterfeit version of them. This is especially true when it comes to crowns. In the introduction to this week, we talked about crowns being symbols of significance and importance. In our world, what do we crown as important and significant?

Money.

Clout.

Fame.

Following your "heart."

Getting even.

Nice cars.

Lavish lifestyles.

Do you think this is what Paul had in mind when he wrote about eternal crowns? Obviously not. Paul was talking about accomplishing our purpose and mission in Christ—making disciples of all nations, loving our neighbor, and serving one another in humility.

But there is still a crown we can wear here on earth, and it's described by Paul in our passage: Jesus Himself. His glory. His joy. *His presence* should be the crown we wear—our most distinguished quality.

As Christians, we have more to be joyful about in this life than anyone else on earth. We've discovered the secret to all life's pain, all future questions, and all current worry: hope in Jesus.

We can't get so distracted by earthly crowns that we fail to don our crowns of glory and joy.

RESPOND

1. What—or who—is Paul's glory and joy? Look up the verses right before 19 and 20 for more context.

2. If you were to describe your earthly crown right now, what would it be like? (It would symbolize your most distinguished characters and qualities.)

3. How would you or your life have to change for you to don a crown of glory and joy? How do you think doing so might benefit you and the ones you love? What earthly crowns would you have to lay down to do so?

ACTIVITY

Let's get creative. Break out the colored pens and design what you think a crown of glory and joy might look like. Don't worry, no one is going to judge your artistic skills!

CHALLENGE

Be cognizant of the crowns of the world in your life. Propose in your heart to keep your eye on the prize—things of the eternal.

REFLECTION

This is our final session together—can you believe it? If you stuck with me all this way, girl, I have to say it—you've shown some grit. I want you to think about all five steps of grit. Can you remember them?

I'll help you out.

Step One: Surrender to God.

Step Two: Listen to the Holy Spirit.

Step Three: Don't conform to the patterns of this world.

Step Four: Turn to the "Who" when you want to ask "Why."

Step Five: Wear that crown, because YOU are more than a conquerer.

Reflect on:

How have I seen myself grow in grit over the past five weeks? (think of a few specific examples)

_____

_____

_____

_____

How does my current state of surrender help me to or hinder me from listening to the Holy Spirit?

_____

_____

_____

_____

In what ways does the Holy Spirit sound different than the voices in this world, and what did I learn in this study that has helped me open my heart to input from the Holy Spirit?

_____

_____

_____

_____

Am I trying to look at "Who" instead of asking "Why"? How am I doing that?

_____

_____

_____

_____

_____

Do my "Why" questions distract me from the race of faith?

_____

_____

_____

_____

How do I want my life to change as a result of growing in God's grit?

_____

_____

_____

_____

How would I explain "grit" to a friend?

_____

_____

_____

_____

ABOUT THE AUTHOR

A Bible teaching, word-slanging, MexiRican who is passionate about raising up a generation of people with hearts longing for Jesus Christ. Bianca was illiterate until the age of twelve and through her grit she chose not to quit and has written three impactful books.

As an author, speaker, and podcaster, she knows the power of words and wields them wisely. As a church planter and industry leader, she is committed to proclaiming the gospel domestically and internationally through her unique personality bringing insightful and powerful teachings.

But why? Because she has seen way too many of her closest friends lose their way, live isolated, and forget their faith just as so many others do.

If Jesus is real, we can be too! It's time to get out of the box, color outside the lines, and live counterculturally.

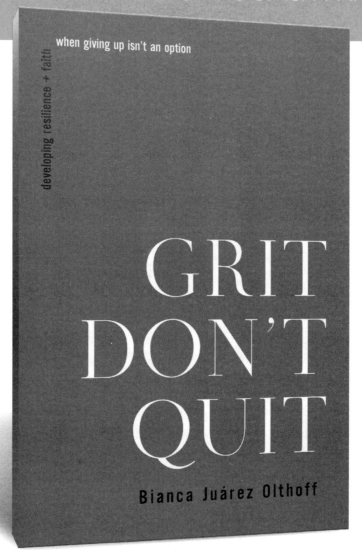

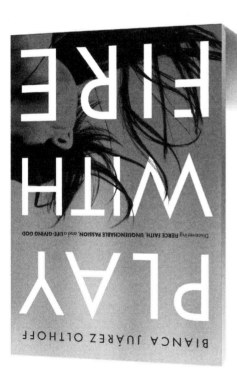

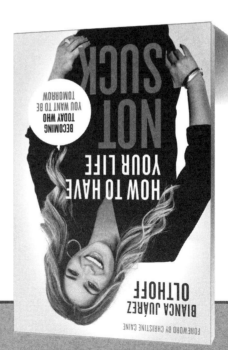